RANDOM TAKES BALTIMORE

An original screenplay

by David Grant

This is a work of fiction. Names, characters, places, and incidents either are the product of the author's imagination or are used fictitiously. Any resemblance to actual persons, living or dead, events or locales is entirely coincidental.

ISBN: 978-0-9992-0848-9

RANDOM TAKES BALTIMORE
is a municipal version of
the national second feature of:
The Common Lot Quartet:

The Fight for Random (#1)
Random Takes Off (#2)
Democracy at Random (#3)
Random Ring (#4)

The *Quartet* imagines a national legislative body that is statistically representative of the entire population. Legislators are chosen as juries are. By random selection.

The first of the *Quartet,* **The Fight for Random**, is a wild magical realist take on how the first legislature-by-the-people comes to be.

The second, **Random Takes Off**, is a realist political action drama, spiced by elements of absurdist satire. [**Random Takes Baltimore** imagines a similar scenario but on the smaller-scale (and probable first step) of a city council.]

The third, **Democracy at Random**, is an unlikely road trip by an odd couple of representatives who advocate, separately, for income redistribution and consumer-driven eugenics.

Random Ring is not yet written.

The scripts are formatted for ebook and print publication, not to film industry specifications.

Although the scripts are in chronological order, they stand independently. A first-time reader might do best to choose by one's preferred genre.

Screenplay formatting terms

CONT'D – Continued. Used when speech is interrupted by narrative description.

CONTINUOUS – Indicates that one scene follows right on the heels of the other, without any jump in time.

EXT. – Exterior. Outdoors. Master scene heading.

EXT./INT. – Scene moves from exterior to interior.

FREEZE FRAME – The image freezes on the screen and becomes a still shot.

INT. – Interior. Inside. Master scene heading.

INTERCARD – A black & white title card, as in old silent movies.

(O.S.) OFF SCREEN – Subject is at the location but not in camera frame.

SHOCK CUT – A sudden cut from one scene to another.

STOCK SHOT – A film sequence previously shot and stored at a film library.

SUPER – A superimposition – one image (usually words) overlaid on another.

(V.O.) Voice Over – A voice that comes through a device such as a telephone or radio or that is heard in the mind.

RANDOM TAKES BALTIMORE

*[Unless otherwise noted,
all scenes are
in Baltimore, Maryland]*

FADE IN:

INT. TELEVISION STUDIO - DAY

The set's marquee reads "Sortition for the People's Platform." MODERATOR directs a girl and a boy to each blindly reach into a box to pull out a numbered ping-pong ball.

In the audience, Baltimore Mayor J. RENARD DAYTON, 60's, African-American, sits with a young INTERN. DAYTON is a slow-talking patrician dinosaur.

> DAYTON: Choice. Holding it on May Day. Making it like bingo. They're going to get away with it. For awhile.

> INTERN: What, Mayor, sir?

> DAYTON: Ritual. Americana. Symbols and signs. Top-notch P-R. They know what they do.

INT. KITCHEN, ASHBURTON NEIGHBORHOOD - CONTINUOUS

SYLVIA LYDA GRESHAM, early 30's, African-Am, dices onions at the sink. She occasionally looks out the window to admire her springtime garden and the leafy green of the upper-middle class neighborhood.

Behind her, in semi-darkness, wheelchair-bound CLARA ADAMS, 50, African-Am, stares intently at the television live broadcast of the "Sortition."

INT. OFFICE OF "ALLWAYS CHURCH OF THE SALVATION" - CONTINUOUS

The Reverend EMMANUEL PACQUINO, 36, Filipino-American, hair slicked, huddles around a television monitor with half dozen advisors, all male, including BAYANI and CRISANTO.

Ostentatious gold crucifixes -- embossed with "Allaw of The Manifest" -- sway from every neck.

Pacquino: compensates for his pipsqueak voice by speaking rapid-fire in an English dominated by his native Tagalog ('b' or 'p' replacing 'f').

>PACQUINO: *Tsch!* Shameful! No respect! Stat-Rep is devil's work.

>BAYANI: Statistical Representation... It's a free rider's paradise.

ON TELEVISION - THE SORTITION EVENT

>PACQUINO (O.S.): Statistical representation is insult. To my family. To all Pinoy. We come here to work hard. To get ahead. Not to lose to the undeserving.

BACK TO SCENE

>CRISANTO: The end of meritocracy.

>PACQUINO: Crisanto, my boy. You know. You know.

Crisanto nods in conspiratorial agreement.

>PACQUINO (CONT'D): They trample The Manifest! They disobey Allaw! Tsch!

2

INT. TV STUDIO - CONTINUOUS

The moderator displays ping-pong balls to the camera: "#135" and "#571." At his left is a computer labelled "ODD - DECAY."

> MODERATOR: This one randomizes by following radioactive decay of a mineral.

To his right, a computer labelled "EVEN - STATIC."

> MODERATOR (CONT'D): This one randomizes by atmospheric static. Our two young people have shown us numbers adding to seven-oh-six, an even number. And so we now begin the sortition. Random Selection for our country's first-ever municipal People's Platform!

> DAYTON (in audience, to Intern): Squeaky clean... With the two innocents. Not bad, not bad.

INT. WAITING ROOM OF PSYCHIATRIST OFFICE - CONTINUOUS

MELVIN "TURKEY" GALILEO POLAT, late 20's, Euro-Am, scrawny, swarthy, bursts into the empty room, picks up the clipboard sign-in sheet and scribbles in the "Name" column: "Turkey".

He restlessly paces, paying no attention to the television broadcasting the "Sortition" event.

ON TELEVISION - SORTITION VIA ATMOSPHERIC
EVENTS

Series of webcams from around the globe: lightning,
tornado, aurora borealis, dust storm, etc.

> MODERATOR (O.S.): These events, plus sunspots
> and cosmic rays, cause radio static. By connecting
> this computer to those signals, purely random
> selection of the fifteen names for the People's
> Platform is assured.

INT. OFFICE OF "ALLWAYS" MEGACHURCH -
CONTINUOUS

> PACQUINO: ...harnessing God-given nature to
> their desecration!

INT. TV STUDIO AUDIENCE - CONTINUOUS

> DAYTON (to Intern): And after the sweet and
> simple, like at a county fair... they bring on the high
> tech. Choice.

> INTERN: Way cool.

> DAYTON: As if the way the numbers were
> generated mattered at all... Disinformation for the
> disinformed.

Intern pouts disappointment.

> DAYTON (CONT'D): Damn fool idea, filling the City
> Council with ordinary, unelected... citizens.

MONTAGE - MECHANISM OF SORTITIONAL SELECTION

-- Computer screen, numbers popping up sporadically

-- Fingers running over numbers correlated to names

-- Letters of invitation to the People's Platform mailed out

EXT. GARDEN, ASHBURTON NEIGHBORHOOD - DAY

Sylvia is harvesting lettuce. In straw hat and print dress, she's as bright and prim as her daisies.

POSTWOMAN drives up and hails her to sign for a letter. Sylvia carries it and the other mail back to the house.

EXT. PORCH OF BUNGALOW - CONTINUOUS

Cathy's disabled aunt Clara wheels herself onto the porch of their Ashburton neighborhood home. Tapping her knee, Clara demands the mail. Sylvia hands over all but one.

> SYLVIA: Registered.

> CLARA: Our banker?

> SYLVIA: Government. For me.

Sylvia holds the door for her aunt to wheel herself in.

INT. BUNGALOW - CONTINUOUS

Sylvia reads her letter while Clara trashes the rest. Sylvia gets up to water a begonia. She lingers at a photo of her parents and herself as a pre-pubescent.

Clara rolls over, glances at the letter. And rejoices.

> CLARA: Congratulations! Celebration! Tea and crumpets... In honor of our royalist ancestors! Sylvia shudders, dismayed.

> SYLVIA: Why recognize those white masters who raped our grandmothers?

> CLARA (sings): It ain't necessarily so.

Clara mimes a wheelchair-bound curtsey.

> CLARA (CONT'D): It's jackpot for us.

> SYLVIA (despondent): Three years. I won't have much time for the garden. I... I... How could I have been chosen?

> CLARA: Luck of the draw. You are. We are!

> SYLVIA: Why did I ever listen to you?

> CLARA: Because I'm your brilliant auntie who knows what's what! We had to make sure we got our fifty-plus percent.

> SYLVIA: Yes, yes. (parroting) Women would not sign up. Especially not black women.

> CLARA (overly cheery): Our chance to deal with potholes, property taxes, affordable housing, re-zoning and...

> SYLVIA: Comparing it to a call to jury duty... But I never expected... What were the odds?

CLARA: About half of the registered voters volunteered for the sortition, for the lottery. That's two hundred and ten thousand. Almost all of them passed the civics test.

SYLVIA: Which wasn't any more difficult than a driver's license test. But I never expected...

CLARA: With fourteen members chosen by district, plus the president city-wide... Your chances were one of out of about a fourteen thousand.

From her blouse, Sylvia withdraws a necklace with a small silver crucifix and bows her head reverently.

CLARA (CONT'D): My God, Sylvia, if anybody can do it, you can. Democracy and humility are twins.

SYLVIA (deep sigh): I don't know, Clara.

INT. "CONFEDERATES' CONTINGENT" OFFICE - DAY

THE ORGANIZER, grizzled grunt, 60, Afro-Am, commands a disheveled desk in the middle of a disheveled office. On the wall behind him, a poster of a green butterfly with the slogan: "Elect = To Pick, To Choose".

"Turkey" slouches on an office sofa. His speech swings erratically between over-heated and tranquil.

THE ORGANIZER: You're the big winner, Melvin.

TURKEY: "Melvin"... Humpf!

THE ORGANIZER: What, you want me to use your nickname?

TURKEY: You got a problem with that?

THE ORGANIZER: I'm just saying...

TURKEY: My Daddy was proud. And a patriot.
Never woulda hung out with confederates.

THE ORGANIZER: The name's to confuse them.
Back in the civil war, Baltimore wanted to secede.
Some still hold the notion that it's a southern city.
(chuckles) Confederate, after all, just means a
brother-in-arms. Nothing to do with north or south.
And by using it, we take it away from those yahoos
waving the old Dixie battle flag.

INT. BASEMENT KITCHEN - NIGHT - FLASHBACK

Turkey's impoverished immigrant FATHER and MOTHER
are arguing. Their INFANT BOY lies on the table between
them. Along with an open copy of *Poor Richard's
Almanac,*.

FATHER (reading): "The turkey is respectable... a
true original native of America." Turkey, better.

MOTHER: We say already. From science name:
Mel-Lea gall-o-pov-a. (stubbornly) Mel, if boy. Lea,
if girl.

FATHER: Melvin, pah! He still gonna be our... little
Turkey!

END FLASHBACK

THE ORGANIZER: Man, just... You could make it
easier on yourself... Coming out of... as you have...

TURKEY: ... the loony bin! Yeah, say it. The
hoosegow. Rehab.

THE ORGANIZER: Maybe you're taking on more than you should?

TURKEY: What, stay cooped? Stuck in that incubator? If I didn't take off, that's where I'd deserve to be.

THE ORGANIZER: You're gonna have enemies.

TURKEY: Yeah. Eagles. Bald-headed rich folk. Papa called them: Carrion eaters.

THE ORGANIZER: Why we organized... You know the story, right?

TURKEY: Lotta time on the inside. For a lotta news. Slick, how you avoided federal intervention.

THE ORGANIZER: Four-to-three with the Maryland Court of Appeals. We were lucky. The swing judge went to Bryn Mawr School, here in the city. The judge admired the school's early headmistress, Edith Hamilton. Hamilton was a classics scholar.

TURKEY: Just like Baltimore. Old money, old thoughts, ancient history...

THE ORGANIZER: The example of the original democracy swayed her. The Athenians did not vote for officials. They chose them by lot. (sizing him up) But now that part of The Contingent's work is done. You on meds?

TURKEY: What? Worried I'm gonna embarrass you? All the effort... and you get a... (over the top) Nut case! Out of the blue! Named Turkey!

The Organizer jumps a little.

THE ORGANIZER: You through with the mushrooms? Peyote? Ayahuasca? Heard you stuck with organics. (denigrating) Some kind of purist?

Turkey blows him off.

THE ORGANIZER (CONT'D): Ten percent of the city is hooked on heroin. Another bunch are coked up or strung out on meth. They may not be purists but... (ironic) You got yourself a built-in constituency.

TURKEY: Think that's funny, hunh? (bristling) You ain't nothin' but another politico. No place for people like me. (tapping his temple) A Glider. A Mind-Glider.

The Organizer rolls his eyes. Waits.

TURKEY (CONT'D) (calmer): Shee... Don't worry, man. My files are sealed. In-vi-o-lable, they said.

THE ORGANIZER (skeptical): Right. (softening) Look, if you find yourself... unduly consternated, shall we say... We're still in business. Behind you. Just a bus ride away.

TURKEY: You think I need coddling?

The Organizer sighs, rises, offers a handshake.

THE ORGANIZER: Highest office in a democracy, y'know? Citizen. How about joining the club?

TURKEY(sloughing it off): Yeah, sure... *Adios, amigo.*

INT. LEXINGTON MARKET - DAY

Tired and groggy, Turkey hauls a bulky duffel up to a food stall.

Behind the counter, Indo-Trinidadian SANJIT AGRAWAL, 35, greets him with a fist bump.

>SANJIT: Going somewhere, mon?

>TURKEY: Scored. Moving up. Gimmie a crab cake.

Sanjit sizes him up.

>SANJIT: Oh yeah? Crab cake? I can't front you no more.

>TURKEY: Not asking for nothing, Sanjit.

As Turkey fumbles for change, Sanjit laughs.

>SANJIT: Messing with you, mon.

He flops a crab cake onto the griddle.

>TURKEY: New day for me. Did you hear? I'm a rep.

>SANJIT: Yeah, I heard. People's Platform.

Sanjit winks and points at his lapel pin, a green butterfly.

>SANJIT (CONT'D): I been in The Contingent for years. So now... You're in power.

He snap-pops his fingers.

SANJIT (CONT'D): Turkey. Congrats. Y'know I always wondered about how you got your name?

TURKEY: My papa admired Ben Franklin.

SANJIT: Yeah? My daddy loved Franklin, too. But people won't take you seriously with that nickname. You gotta get serious.

Turkey notices a nearby magazine rack. The cover of a wrestling magazine catches his eye: "The Terrible Turk".

TURKEY: Okay... How about "Turk"? How about... I'm from a family of wrestlers?

The new "Turk" straightens up, bold and cold.

Turkey (CONT'D): I'll grow a mustache. I... am... ferocious! Wild!

SANJIT: There you go, mon! With wild comes free.

INT. "THE BARBARIAN" SPORTS BAR - DAY

Mayor Dayton and Reverend Pacquino sit on stools bombarded by screens of football. Dayton fondles a martini, Pacquino nurses a half-and-half (iced tea and lemonade).

DAYTON: Your, ah, Movement for Repentance?

PACQUINO (reverential): On Our Knees For All The People.

DAYTON: You're more American than all of us, Rev. Fasting and prayer. Original values, back to Washington and Adams. (snickering) Politics and piety.

PACQUINO: We develop strategy. We make movement. In Tagalog we say: *Ako na!* I-Will-Be-The-One!

The Mayor's attention diverts to the television.

Football gladiators head-bang in slo-mo.

DAYTON: Delectable. (measured) Reverend, what the people crave is story. With winners. And losers. None of this win-win dreck.

He ponders his glass, toasts Pacquino.

DAYTON (CONT'D): Your forté. A sermon, a parable. With a moral at its end.

Pacquino responds to the toast, raising his lemonade.

PACQUINO: Terrorists Manifest the Evil One!

Dayton winces. Downs the martini. Stares into space.

DAYTON: Granddaddy.

PACQUINO: What?

EXT. SWIMMING POOL - DAY – DAYTON"S MEMORY

Mid-1920's, summertime at Baltimore's large public swimming pool. Posted "Whites Only". DAYTON'S GRANDFATHER, 15, cleans the toilets.

When he sees another boy, also African-American, outside the fence, Dayton's Grandfather roughly shoos the boy away.

The Boy walks away, distressed, as Dayton's Grandfather smiles cruelly at him.

BACK TO SCENE

> DAYTON: A story. With a moral. One about himself that Grandaddy gave me. He shakes himself out of it.

> DAYTON (CONT'D): But no matter... Might you be acquainted, Reverend, with infrasound?

Pacquino eyeballs Dayton suspiciously.

> DAYTON (CONT'D): Psycho-acoustics. Waves below seventeen hertz, we hear nothing. But we're hard-wired to shiver. Earplugs don't work. It goes right to the bones. Sure-fire fright.

> PACQUINO: But if one's faith is strong, *Tsch*!

> DAYTON: Friends of mine, people in the business so to say... invited me to a demonstration. Part of the federal government's R-and-D.

Dayton points to the ring he wears on his left index finger, a green emerald surrounded by tiny diamonds.

> DAYTON (CONT'D): My grandfather's. It started jumping, buzzing. Burning. Everybody crawled right out of there.

> PACQUINO: Faith does not matter?

Dayton pulls out his smart phone and taps up a video.

ON SMART PHONE - INFRASOUND DEMONSTRATION

A laboratory. In the room's center, a metal rod upright. Standing, back to the walls, the Mayor, technicians and unknown well-dressed others.

14

DAYTON (O.S.): Keep your eye on that rod.

The rod begins to vibrate.

DAYTON (O.S.) (CONT'D): We heard nothing.

Everyone in the lab begins shivering, shrinking, slinking out the door.

DAYTON (O.S.): (CONT'D): Those waves can also be tuned to resonate with your eyeball. Images appear.

PACQUINO (O.S.): Hallucinations.

BACK TO SCENE

DAYTON: Your territory, Reverend.

He shrugs.

DAYTON (CONT'D): Call in your exorcists.

PACQUINO (enthusiastic): We manufacture fear!

DAYTON: You handle the believers. My people will handle the rest. Belief must balance with reason.

PACQUINO (darkly): Your people must become believers. Reason is a tool of the Evil One.

DAYTON: Is that so, Reverend? (dismissive) Well now... about The Movement. You have, I pray, disciples willing to starve in front of the cameras?

PACQUINO: We are arranging...

DAYTON: Good. We need them struggling against turpitude. And degradation.

PACQUINO: Mayor, my people came to Baltimore... as to New Jerusalem. But we have seen now the danger. (comically sincere) And We-Will-Be-The-One!

DAYTON: Not to worry, Reverend. The People's Platform is incapable of sacrifice. It will produce nothing but comedy. Of the most plebeian sort.

ON TELEVISION - FOOTBALL MANIA

The crowd. The cheerleaders. The game.

DAYTON (O.S.): Indeed, Reverend, the danger is... our own people. They need heroes, they need chiefs.

PACQUINO (O.S.): Thank God we still elect you. The executive. The One-Who-Knows.

BACK TO SCENE

Dayton beats his chest, self-deprecating, gorilla-style.

DAYTON: Ki-mo-sabe.

PACQUINO: is flummoxed.

Dayton laughs and points above the bar to a replica of "The Dying Gaul", an ancient statue of a naked warrior.

PACQUINO (shuddering): Disgusting! *Tsch!*

DAYTON (at the statue): They knew how to die.

INT. CITY HALL CONFERENCE ROOM - DAY

The fifteen new representatives and their fifteen assistants attend the orientation session. TURK (former "Turkey"), Sylvia and Clara sit in separate parts of the room. An INSTRUCTOR goes over Rules of Order and Decorum.

> INSTRUCTOR: During debate each Councilman must... (catches herself) Excuse me... Each Platform Member must... avoid personal references to any other member.

She points at the list of "Platform Rules" projected on an overhead screen and reads them:

> INSTRUCTOR (O.S.): (CONT'D): "No eating, drinking or smoking" "No phones or laptops" "Unobtrusive Handhelds OK" Timidly, Sylvia raises her hand.

> SYLVIA: How about praying? Is that allowed?

Other representatives jerk around to see her.

> INSTRUCTOR: Um? Other than an invocation to open a session, no. No prayer rugs, no getting down on your knees. Secular decorum only, please.

> SYLVIA: There are many forms of prayer. Thank you.

The Instructor moves on.

> INSTRUCTOR: You've got seventy-some pages of rules handed down to you from the previous city council. Read them.

She lifts up a hardbound copy of *Robert's Rules of Order.*

> INSTRUCTOR (CONT'D): Anything else you want to know about how to proceed is in here.

She thumps the book.

> INSTRUCTOR (CONT'D): This is your baby.

Clara raises her hand and is recognized. She speaks firmly.

> CLARA: Our baby? Maybe, ma'am, you've been here too long. Maybe the Peoples Platform wants to run its meetings differently.

> INSTRUCTOR: (peeved): It's been this way...

> CLARA: It's been run on a basis of patriarchal hierarchy.

> INSTRUCTOR: I guess you don't need me.

The Instructor summarily walks out.

INT. CHAMBER OF THE PEOPLE'S PLATFORM - DAY

Early January, opening session of the first sortitionally-selected "People's Platform."

Of the fifteen reps, eight are women, seven men. Nine are Afro-Am; four, Euro-Am; one Latino; and one Asian. Four under 35 years old; four in middle age; three over 55.

Five are dressed in the uniforms of low-wage service jobs. Five are in middle-class-motley. A couple wear business casual. One is in coat and tie. One's t-shirt does not cover jeans hanging down past his butt crack.

A group of representatives -- WORKING CLASS MALE, MIDDLE CLASS MALE, MIDDLE CLASS FEMALE -- cluster to the side.

> WORKING CLASS MALE: That session about Plats and Plans had my head spinning.

> MIDDLE CLASS FEMALE: I didn't know every new Council... er, Platform... can make its own rules.

> MIDDLE CLASS MALE: As long as we properly conduct ourselves...

> MIDDLE CLASS FEMALE (prissy): Maybe we should have been more strict about the dress code.

> WORKING CLASS MALE: Not everybody can afford...

> MIDDLE CLASS MALE (interrupting): Clothes or no clothes... Each to his own.

> WORKING CLASS MALE (jokey): No clothes? We gonna see streakers?

> MIDDLE CLASS FEMALE: That would rather fail the decorum test, would it not?

> MIDDLE CLASS MALE: Lighten up, lady. It takes all kinds.

> WORKING CLASS MALE: Gotta thank the Law of Large Numbers. Sortition accomplished what it promised.

> MIDDLE CLASS MALE: Stat-Rep, statistical representation. Nothing can be fairer, more equitable.

WORKING CLASS MALE: Ain't so that it's identity politics. Nah... It's government by the people. Finally...

MIDDLE CLASS FEMALE: If... we can keep it?

INT. "RUTH'S DINER" - DAY

Sanjit and Turk at the counter. Behind it, RUTH, mid-50s, a smile as wide as her two hundred pounds. On the television behind them, another football game.

RUTH: And you are...?

TURK (TURKEY): Turk. Turk Polat, ma'am.

RUTH: So. A politician.

SANJIT: Not. Not, Babe. Not a politician.

RUTH: Oh yeah. The Revolution. Baltimore's contribution to the-next-step-for-democracy. (head shake) Or, some customers say: The Catastrophe. That sortition thing. Aggie, I'll stick with the sports pages.

Sanjit lifts up a copy of *The Baltimore Sun* from the counter.

SANJIT: Surprises, Babe. Surprises coming. Better watch a headline or two.

RUTH: With all of Baltimore's problems -- homicides, poverty double the national average, blight...

SANJIT: Exactly! What has the city got to lose? Why not be a forerunner?

RUTH (pointing to Turk): How'd you hook up with...? You still hanging out in that mess of an office with the Contingent?

SANJIT: Random is as random does, Babe. I'm his deputy.

He flexes non-existent muscle, then taps his skull.

SANJIT (CONT'D): Brains behind the brawn.

RUTH: So, Aggie, you finally get to use some of that highfalutin' education. (glances at Turk) Turk, hey? A Young Turk.

SANJIT (dead-pan): He's from a family of Anatolian wrestlers.

Turk smiles humbly and picks a pretzel out of a jar.

TURK (to Ruth, nonchalant): How come he calls you Babe?

RUTH (laughs): My name's Ruth.

TURK (oblivious): Yeah? And...

RUTH: Never mind.

TURK: They tell me I'm entering the heart of some beast.

Ruth motions to the televised football game.

RUTH (to Sanjit): I'm still sticking with my religion.

TOM MOORE, 50, Euro-Am, craggy, wearing a hard hat, ambles over behind Sanjit and slaps him on the shoulders.

TOM MOORE: Religious ecstasy, hey, Ruth?

Sanjit does not turn to see who it is.

SANJIT (to Turk): That's not a hard hat. It's his head.

RUTH" (to Tom Moore): You going to let him get away with that?

TOM MOORE (jocular): I believe that assault on a municipal officer is a felony. Anyway, nobody's laying odds.

RUTH: Money, money, money... you still blowing wages at the Horseshoe?

TOM MOORE (to Sanjit): Congratulations, Sanjit. So the Confederates' Contingent didn't set it up? You just fell into it?

Moore reaches out to shake hands with Turk but Turk mistakes his intention and hands Moore a pretzel.

TOM MOORE (CONT'D) (covering the gaff): Unh. Pleased to meet you. (to Sanjit) Listen to her, the sports fan. And she doesn't think about money!

ON TELEVISION - FOOTBALL

SANJIT (O.S.): Vikings, the originals... they kicked a skull from one village to another. Victory celebrations. And thus came football, soccer and rugby.

BACK TO SCENE

>TOM MOORE: Careful that doesn't happen to you and your young boss.

>SANJIT: No victory celebrations?

>TOM MOORE: Avoid the guillotine.

INT. "ACOLYTES OF ADAM" STOREFRONT CHURCH – NIGHT

Sepia-skinned PREACHER ALMA JOHNSON, 50s, Afro-Am, concludes exhorting her CONGREGATION, an eclectic mix of pigmentations and wardrobes.

>PREACHER JOHNSON (vigorously): ... and we thank God! For His divine intervention! Upon that random generator machine! Bringing us this fine young Platform Representative... Jas Robinson!

In a front pew, JAS ROBINSON, 30, Afro-Am, in an oversized black suit, rises half-way, then recedes.

>PREACHER JOHNSON (CONT'D): And now a guest from our suburban brethren at Allways Church of the Salvation... the Reverend Emmanuel Pacquino!

Pacquino bounds to the altar amidst Hosanna's and Amen's.

>PACQUINO: Thank you, Jesus! Thank you for helping this young Representative! Making good on his chance. His task is daunting. The task we all face. But he. And we. Will-Be-The-One!

Murmurs and mild shouts of assent.

23

PACQUINO (CONT'D): Sacrifice! Sacrifice means To-Make-Holy! That's why we are here tonight. To make holy. To make ourselves holy. Our friends holy. Our families holy. Our neighborhood. Our city. Holy!

Pacquino holds a pause, drops an octave.

PACQUINO (CONT'D): On the other hand... We hear the word: Sortition... It comes from Latin... *Sors*.

He shoots a surreptitious accusing glance at Johnson. She flinches.

PACQUINO (CONT'D) (full blast): That leads to... Sorcery!

CONGREGATION (lamentations): Oh Lord! / Please, God, please! / Help us, Lord! / Have mercy!

PACQUINO: We must repent. The city must repent. A Movement for Repentance! Of fasting. Of prayer.

CONGREGATION: Amen. Amen. Amen. Yes! Yes! Yes!

INT. VESTRY OF THE ACOLYTES CHURCH - LATER

A Black Madonna statue stands in the corner. At its feet: a bundle of herbs, incense sticks, fresh fruit, canned food and a black hawk's feather.

Pacquino gives Johnson a box with a label obviously re-used: "Brain Science Institute/Johns Hopkins School of Medicine." He opens it to show its contents -- switches and dials and speakers.

> PACQUINO: One of my parishioners... His name is Crisanto... He will help you set it up.

Pacquino points to the statue.

> PACQUINO (CONT'D) (insinuating): You haven't given it up?

> PREACHER JOHNSON: It shouldn't offend you.

> PACQUINO: Our largesse only goes so far.

> PREACHER JOHNSON (slyly accusing): Your mother would approve.

Pacquino glares.

> PREACHER JOHNSON (CONT'D): More than one of my buffalo soldier boys would approve. Too. (threatening) Subic Bay was... quite a place, so they say.

INT. CHAMBER OF THE PEOPLE'S PLATFORM - DAY

Carrying a folder, Sylvia squirms into a seat farthest from the podium. Clara's wheelchair is pulled up close by.

The gavel pounds, mumblings diminish. A Jewish chaplain completes the invocation.

THE CHAIR, 50, Afro-Am, female, opens the floor.

> THE CHAIR: As we decided in orientation, we are adopting a practice of the federal lower house.

From her place in the front row, representative IRIS REID, Euro-Am, 30's, petite and proper, rises and addresses the room in a voice both timid and precise.

> IRIS REID: Madam Chair, I ask unanimous consent to address the Platform for one minute and to revise and extend my remarks.

> THE CHAIR: Without objections, so ordered.

Ignoring the proceedings, Sylvia slips from her folder the Rawlings Conservatory's listing of flora available for municipal offices.

Clara focuses on the speeches, paying no attention to Sylvia.

SYLVIA'S DAYDREAMING - HER GARDEN AT HOME

She's piddling happily among a bed of herbs.

BACK TO SCENE

> IRIS REID: ... and why should we representatives stand to gain so much from the happenstance of our selection? We're servants of the people, aren't we? Seventy-thousand dollars is a lot of money for most of us. About twenty thousand more than Baltimore's mean household income. I propose a reduction.

SYLVIA'S DAYDREAMING - FOREST CRUCIFIXION

A pre-pubescent Sylvia is crucified on a blossoming dogwood tree. She looks down upon the automobile accident that killed her parents and crippled her aunt. Her dead mother's hand grasps the silver crucifix Sylvia now wears.

26

BACK TO SCENE

The Chair recognizes "the lady from District Four."
ANTONIA BALDWIN, 50's, Euro-Am, matronly, poised,
clears her throat.

> ANTONIA BALDWIN: My forebears established the
> Domino Sugar company. The concern thrived
> because of immigrants.

SYLVIA'S DAYDREAMING - THERAPY POOL

Sylvia eases Clara out of her wheelchair into sulfurous
waters of an outdoor spa. The sun shines, a warm breeze
blows. Sylvia floats languidly as a therapist manipulates
Clara's useless legs.

> ANTONIA BALDWIN (O.S.): The Universal
> Declaration of Human Rights provides the right of
> asylum from persecution. You would think, given
> the Lady up there in the New York Harbor, that we
> would want to honor that.

SYLVIA'S DAYDREAMING - IMMIGRANTS

Sylvia imagines immigrants transiting Ellis Island. The
faces morph into representatives of the People's Platform.

> ANTONIA BALDWIN (O.S.): Those who believe we
> should close our doors deny our history and our
> values. Let us declare that our city welcomes those
> who are yearning to breathe free.

BACK TO SCENE

Baldwin sits down. Sylvia blinks, opens her eyes, turns to
see Clara glaring at her.

27

The CHAIR (O.S.): The Chair recognizes the gentleman from District Fourteen.

CLIFF SMITH, Euro-American, 40, rises to claim his one-minute. A gaudy turquoise bracelet encircles his wrist.

CLIFF SMITH: Madam Chair, my proposal challenges the character and the tradition of Baltimorean leadership. It has to do with the way we approach the homicide rate.

As he speaks Cliff holds up photos, one after the other, of:

-- an atomic bomb detonation;
-- a missile-firing submarine;
-- a B-2 stealth bomber;
-- a Predator drone.

Sylvia fidgets, goes back to looking at the catalogue of flowers. Clara is entranced by Smith's speech.

CLIFF SMITH (O.S.) (CONT'D): In our schools we teach conflict resolution. But as soon as those pupils walk out, they see nothing but glorification of militaristic might-makes-right.

A LANKY MAN stands up in the gallery.

LANKY MAN: No denigration of the services!

The Chair pounds the gavel. The man remains on his feet.

CLIFF SMITH (ignoring the man): I propose we go beyond community policing. To policing by the community. Without weapons.

LANKY MAN: Absurd. Who is this guy?

The Chair pounds again, summoning police.

> LANKY MAN (CONT'D): I guess you want Bobbies? What kind of...?

Under his breath he utters obscenities.

Sylvia turns around towards him.

> SYLVIA (firm, sharp): Watch your manners.

The Chair summons police, calls for recess and clears the chamber.

MINUTES LATER

Sylvia and Clara make their way through City Hall's gilded corridors.

> SYLVIA (mewling): You know what it's like for me, auntie. Inside. Harnessed. Caged. What a price... The air we breathe here downtown...

> CLARA: Yes, we face three years of sacrifice. But what an opportunity. And... (affecting a tough guy) Look, lady, ya seen this cripple dribble a basketball. Ya know she can wheel. You...! You got ta deal. Get used to it!

EXT. CAMDEN YARDS BASEBALL STADIUM - DAY

On a cold bright April day, Mayor Dayton sits in a warm sky box with red-headed, mini-skirted, up-talking JILL LASULI, 30, Euro-Am. An American flag pin floats on her prominent breast. She has a bit of a lisp, made worse by chewing gum.

LASULI: You, like, want my Representative to get onboard? Got to stir her passion! We go way back. Like, I know her? As kids we called ourselves the Tweetie Birds?

On the field, an infielder muffs an easy grounder.

DAYTON: Must be money on this game. That error was no more random than...

LASULI: Than you and me sitting here?

DAYTON: Most decidedly.

LASULI: One of the guys, in orientation, he said, like, random might be a statistical mirage?

DAYTON: A mirage, you are not.

LASULI: Ain't it... Isn't it that the Reverend preaches that everything is, like, already determined, all locked up?

DAYTON: Dreary. If true, we might as well throw bones. Now, Miss Staff Director for the Honorable Iris Reid... About stirring the passion of your boss?

LASULI: Like I said, us Tweeties fall for the warm and fuzzy. I tell her the re-zoning will, like, protect her high-spirited equine friends? From turning into dog food? Or whatever? She will... P-I-H-P!

DAYTON: Translation, please.

LASULI: Piss. In. Her. Pants.

Lasuli shoots her elbow into his ribs.

LASULI (CONT'D): HAWR! HAWR! HAWR!

Dayton laughs along. Sort of. A little.

>DAYTON: Just make sure, in committee, she keeps it buried. Invisible.

>LASULI: Nice thing about the People's Platform, like, no more us-versus-them? No more party lines. No more, like, yin-yang? Like, Iris is out there, floating? With only me... for a guide?

>DAYTON: Lucky her.

>LASULI: I'm an American Dreamer too, y'know? Iris, she's different. She's complaining about her own salary, that it's too high! Can you imagine? She's the one for causes. I let her fiddle. Keeps her busy?

>DAYTON (anything but): Impressive.

>LASULI: How you gonna keep the neighborhood association quiet? Even if you pay them off, there's always snitches.

>DAYTON: There are forty-seven liquor stores in that neighborhood. You think they want to go elsewhere? Alcohol is their fruit, legal addiction.

Dayton hails a vendor to buy popcorn.

>LASULI: What d'ya get out of it, Mayor? What do you care for the horses, really?

EXT. SWIMMING POOL – DAY - DAYTON'S MEMORY

Back to the 1920's. Dayton's grandfather stands inside the pool's fence, cooly observing the pool's white manager, on the outside of the fence, brutally beating the same African-American boy seen previously.

As the boy slinks away, Dayton's grandfather-as-a-boy shouts, taunting.

>DAYTON'S GRANDFATHER (to the boy): I told you! I told you!

The manager returns inside to Dayton's grandfather, wrapping his arm over the boy's shoulder. Too warmly.

BACK TO SCENE

>DAYTON: Let's just say that it's well and good that you direct Platform Member Reid to worry about... species. I, on the other hand, must worry about... specie. My own. For campaigns. I still have to face voters, remember?

>LASULI (bratty): Life is hard.

>DAYTON: We have to harvest that specie. Always more specie. Fruit.

He hands her the bag of popcorn. She stuffs her mouth.

>DAYTON (CONT'D): We'll take care of your Tweetie Bird's warm-and-fuzzy.

Lasuli crosses her legs in mock offense.

DAYTON (CONT'D): Louche, Ms. Lasuli. That's what you are. Louche Lasuli. Yes.

LASULI: Oh?

DAYTON: Disreputably appealing, louche. It's my specialty. As an aesthete of decay.

LASULI: What a barrel of laughs you are. So what's the price for this deal?

Dayton turns back to the playing field.

DAYTON: As if we weren't on the verge of counter-revolution...

LASULI: At a baseball game?

DAYTON: Welcome to the big leagues. Where there is no repentance possible. Not for any error.

INT. CAFETERIA IN CITY HALL – LATER

Honchos, their aides and extraneous others compete for grub. A menu board reads "May Day Special!"

Clara wheels herself while Sylvia carries a wicker lunch basket to a seat with curtained sunlight.

Turk and Sanjit, carrying their trays, hunt a space. Passing a table of suits, men and women, Turk loudly comments on their meal.

TURK: Hmmm! Carrion salad!

The suits cower for a moment, but Sanjit covers for Turk with an obsequious smile. He then steers Turk towards empty seats where Sylvia and Clara are sitting.

SANJIT: Mind if we join you?

SYLVIA: We're getting used to cramped quarters.

SANJIT: Nice basket. Homemade?

SYLVIA: It's a Wakefield. Victorian. From my grandmother.

CLARA: To my sister.

SYLVIA: My mother.

SANJIT: So... auntie and niece?

Clara confirms. Turk plops down, ignoring the women, and nervously surveys the cafeteria's clientele.

SANJIT (CONT'D): So how's it going? This time, last year, were you watching the sortition on TV? Fascinating...

Before either woman can reply, Turk butts in, prickly.

TURK: Like a county hoosegow in here. Veneer over the same old beef. Meat packers lugging heat.

Sylvia and Clara titter uncertainly.

TURK (CONT'D): Stuffy. Closed. Controlled. Sold.

CLARA: Unh, yes. We'd rather be outdoors. Unh... Too.

TURK (aggressive): Sure you would. I'll bet. What's your game here? Easy-chair lady warriors, hunh?

Sylvia straddles fright and fascination.

SYLVIA: I'm... a gardener.

Turk's eyes dart.

SYLVIA (CONT'D): What about you?

TURK (angry): My folks scratched dirt. Truck farmers. The G-M-O fellahs came along. Seed patents. Wiped them out.

SYLVIA (trying to be helpful): Gregor Mendel was a priest. Life was sacred to him. He never would have...

TURK: Bacterial warfare, is what it is! Transgenic modification. Dangerous? The word is: Omnicidal!

Clara is silenced, Sylvia confused.

SANJIT: Pardon him. He was bottled up for a whole year.

TURK (heated): After they lost their little plot, Papa worked the slaughterhouse. Bottom of the barrel. Immigrant labor.

SANJIT: Testosterone bubbles...

TURK: Bottom of the barrel, because he wanted to grow some beans!

Sanjit places his hand on Turk's shoulder, trying to calm him down. Without effect.

TURK (CONT'D): Yeah, ladies. I'm bottled up! Too many damn Glad-to-meet-you's. Too many "constituents..." Resolutions of Happy Birthday to ninety-year-olds. Blah-blah-blah. This, that...

Turk slams his hand on the table, upsetting their drinks.

Sylvia quietly arises and places their lunch, one item at a time, back into the basket.

> SYLVIA: Good day, gentlemen. Perhaps some other time... (coldly, to Turk) In armchairs, perhaps?

INT. HEADQUARTERS FOR THE MOVEMENT FOR REPENTANCE - DAY

High up in a downtown office enthusiastic operatives stare at computers displaying splashy graphics with slogans.

ON COMPUTER SCREENS

> "End The Reign of Randomness!"
> "Students for Sanity!"
> "Grandmothers for Choice!"
> "Baltimore for Those Who Earned It!"

Dayton and Pacquino wander from station to station, stopping to ask questions of OPERATIVES.

> DAYTON: Did you get the story out on that representative with a fondness for kink?

> CHUBBY OPERATIVE: We gave it to that new rag, *The Baltimore Beat*. They ran it verbatim.

> DAYTON: But that little independent has no credibility.

> CHUBBY OPERATIVE: All the more play when *The Sun* finds it's true.

> DAYTON (light bulb!): Sweet.

Dayton and Pacquino move on to another cubicle.

GANGLY OPERATIVE: Where'd these sitting ducks come from? That whackadoodle for instance, the Anatolian wrestler.

The operative waves Turk's medical records.

GANGLY OPERATIVE (CONT'D): Lost himself in the Strawberry Fields. Grew up on a truck farm but his parents lost it. What do we do with the files?

DAYTON: Into the vaults. Later, if needed. What else?

GANGLY OPERATIVE: Sylvia Gresham's naïveté. An easy mark. And Representative Baldwin, free marketer libertarian for open door immigration. They ought to arrest her for self-mutilation.

PACQUINO: And the no-army guy. His neck is already in a noose.

GANGLY OPERATIVE: Take a look.

ON COMPUTER - BACK TO EARLY 1990'S

A YOUNG CLIFF SMITH circles in a protest line at McKeldin Square. His placard reads "Organic Order: a.k.a. Anarchy."

Other protestors offer 35 mm film canisters to whomever will take them. Wrapped around each canister: "No Blood for Oil!"

GANGLY OPERATIVE (O.S.): On Facebook he rants about... Get this...

Smith puts down the sign and begins, along with other picketers, to disrobe. He stops to display a list to the camera, titled: "One Hundred And Ninety-Eight Methods Of Nonviolent Action."

> YOUNG CLIFF SMITH: Yes, brothers and sisters, it's number twenty-two: Protest Disrobing!

> DAYTON (O.S.): One of our more creative ordinary citizens.

> YOUNG CLIFF SMITH: I threw the *Ching* last night and it came up Number Twenty-Two: Persona. About taking off masks.

Cliff Smith and his cohorts are down to underwear.

> DAYTON (O.S.): Enough of that.

BACK TO SCENE

> GANGLY OPERATIVE: Some kind of anarchist he is, using hocus-pocus from imperial China.

> DAYTON: If he had to face the electorate we'd never have to entertain his drivel.

> Dayton and Pacquino move on to a conference room where strategists contemplate a whiteboard full of scribble.

> SENIOR STRATEGIST: Push lurkers to become commentators. Commentators to forwarders. Forwarders to show-uppers.

> JUNIOR STRATEGIST: Volume isn't the only thing. Content. Intent. Contextual data. It all matters.

DAYTON (annoyed): Gentlemen, don't forget the vernacular! It may be far-fetched, here in beleaguered Baltimore, but we're on the verge of a totalitarian tyranny of the majority! (threatening): Make. Them. Shit. With fear. Of each other.

The strategists are silenced, sheepish, looking one to the other. Finally, the Junior hazards a tentative remark.

JUNIOR STRATEGIST: Police reform? With the lower class now fully represented in the Platform, they'll be calling for more rehabilitation, less retribution.

SENIOR STRATEGIST (not to be upstaged): Right! They'll be screeching for enlightened, progressive... In the vernacular, sir, crap!

JUNIOR STRATEGIST: The numbers are incontrovertible. The uglier the experience in lock-up, the more that criminals straighten up. To avoid going there.

SENIOR STRATEGIST (blustering): People know where it's safe to walk and where it's not.

JUNIOR STRATEGIST: The incarceration rate here in Baltimore is, like the rest of the United States, greater than every other country in the world.

SENIOR STRATEGIST: We need to keep it that way!

JUNIOR STRATEGIST: We've been thinking about planting worst-case-scenarios in... Did you hear about *The Baltimore Beat*?

Dayton and Pacquino chuckle appreciatively.

SENIOR STRATEGIST (taking credit): Wait till you see the *Enquirer*.

ON COMPUTER TABLET - HEADLINE OF THE NATIONAL ENQUIRER

"Unleashing the Barbarians!"

EXT. FORT MCHENRY MONUMENT & PARK - DAY

Turk flies a kite in light wind. Sitting nearby on a blanket, Sanjit reads aloud the *Enquirer* from his tablet.

SANJIT: "... unleashing the barbarians... The criminal genetic footprint is unable to quickly degrade the nerve transmitters involved in arousal..."(guffaws) Could be any young chap with a boner.

He lays the device on the ground.

SANJIT (CONT'D): First *The Beat* for the locals and now it goes national. There's a rumor that this story was leaked from Hopkins, from their Brain Institute. Mainstream media, scooped. Cleared the fact checkers.

Turk's eyes are on his kite, painted as a blue rose with a tail of crepe paper thorns.

TURK (spiky): Criminal? Bribery's criminal. I got an offer. The other day. Fat one.

SANJIT: You what?

TURK: Guy from The Movement For Repentance. Name of Crisanto. Tried to soften me up with some 'shrooms. Said he works at Fort Detrick. Access to all kinds of mind gliders.

40

SANJIT: And?

TURK: Naaww. Been there, done that. But the guy knew what to offer...

A family of TOURISTS stops to admire the kite. Svelte MOTHER, ripped FATHER, three children. All dressed, variously, in orange. Their LITTLE GIRL, an ebony-skinned anomaly among the blondes, bubbles questions.

LITTLE GIRL: Why does it stay up? Can it reach the sky? What makes the string disappear? Why does it wobble?

Turk goes back to his kite. Sanjit turns tour guide.

SANJIT (to the girl): It's sort of like the People's Platform. They meet in City Hall. It looks like a big building downtown.

The girl attends to him, wide-eyed.

SANJIT (CONT'D): But it's held up by an invisible wind.

TOURIST FATHER: Yeah, windbags. (at the girl, kindly) So many questions, daughter.

LITTLE GIRL: But, Daddy, wind is... invisible.

SANJIT: That's right. The wind is like a conception. You know what a conception is?

LITTLE GIRL: The Virgin Mary had one of those... 'Maculate.

SANJIT (touched): The nuns told me about that, too.

The girl eyes the kite up high.

> SANJIT (CONT'D): It is like the wind. You can't see it but you can feel it.

> LITTLE GIRL: Oh?

> SANJIT: The people who keep that City Hall building standing... They represent all the people in this who-o-ole big city. Together we all hold it up... even though you can't see us doing it.

> TOURIST MOTHER (sour): Out where we live, Garrett County, people got a different feeling 'bout government. Except your mayor.

> Turk attaches a green paper butterfly to the kite string.

> SANJIT (to the mother): Dayton and his ilk? That clique?

> TOURIST MOTHER: Ilk, is it? We get your news. W-C-B-M radio, on internet. We hope he runs for governor. Mayor Dayton is one of the few patriots left!

Turk opens the butterfly's wings, admires it.

> TOURIST FATHER: It's rigged, that People's Platform. The Mayor's right, trying to repeal the law.

Turk releases the butterfly and it glides up the string.

TOURIST FATHER (CONT'D): Damn Maryland's Court of Appeals. Relying on that... et-ee-mo-lah... et-ee-...logical dictionary. Pah! Election...? Includes selection...? By sortition? (spits) Lawyers... Judges...

LITTLE GIRL: Mama! Look at the butterfly!

Turk's butterfly reaches the kite, its wings snap shut, and it glides back down to its keeper.

Turk smiles at the girl and taps his temple.

TOURIST FATHER: And if the Mayor and the Reverend fail here in the city... There are other means...

He takes the hand of his little daughter.

TOURIST FATHER (CONT'D) (bragging, sort of): Come on, our little adoptee. (to Turk & Sanjit) Get on out to Deep Creek. You'll see people who know what's going on here in old Body-More. (darkly) An Orange Array...

The father leads the family away.

TURK (to Sanjit): Criminals.

INT. CHAMBER OF THE PEOPLE'S PLATFORM - DAYS LATER - DAY

The Chair is running through a list of pro forma votes. About bus fares, about nuisance noise, about sidewalk repair, etc.

The legalist patter is background noise for Sylvia and Turk. They sit next to other, registering lackadaisical voice votes of "Aye", as needed.

TURK (to Sylvia): How many times we gotta vote on these bills?

SYLVIA: Following procedure is necessary. (responding to Chair) Aye.

TURK: Sorry about the other day. Dyspepsia, I guess.

SYLVIA (frosty): We had not eaten yet.

Turk turns away. Surveys the room, a couple dozen onlookers. And half a dozen video cameras on tripods.

TURK: It's like we're in a boxing ring. Bare knuckled dialectics, that's what they want. (responding to Chair) Aye.

SYLVIA: Bottled up, you said. Pressured by constituents. What constituents?

TURK: Telephone calls. Beggars. Window washers. Small time dealers. (dismissive) Never mind... Aye... Anybody, unh, from The Movement... make you an offer?

SYLVIA: An offer?

TURK: Just wondering.

SYLVIA: This voting in public makes me... feel exposed. Almost naked. Like someone peeking. Discourteous... (to the Chair) Aye.

TURK: Discourteous? Man, this bunch is way more courteous than its predecessor... Aye... They had to campaign, to compete, to butt heads...

SYLVIA (heated): Oh, so now you are defending election campaigns? You want to return to your old haunts? Is it too much trouble for you, the responsibility of public office?

TURK (meeting her heat): The armchair lady's got dander up? Oooweee!

SYLVIA (another notch up): You're just like your kites. Any which way the wind blows... Aye.

TURK: At least I know which way the... (deleting the expletive) ... wind blows.

SYLVIA: I should have known better than to befriend someone of such flighty pedigree.

TURK: Oh, flighty, is it...? Aye.

SYLVIA: Unstable. I'll take the arm chair. Over your flights of fancy.

TURK: Ever been up? In a balloon?

SYLVIA: No. And I don't want to.

TURK: Afraid of the wind?

SYLVIA: You're insufferable.

They simmer in stalemate.

SYLVIA (CONT'D): Aye.

EXT. INNER HARBOR - DAY

Dayton and Pacquino walk along the wharf near the *U.S.S. Constellation*.

DAYTON: Mass Sociogenic Illness...

PACQUINO: Possible? To induce... hysteria?

Dayton points over to McKeldin Square.

DAYTON: Baltimore Riot of 1861 took place there. First fatal casualty of the civil war happened right there.

PACQUINO: They did not have time, those men. To succumb. To hysteria.

Dayton rubs his emerald ring. Troubled, nervous.

DAYTON: For an individual, hysteria can come quick. Especially for one who considers himself superior.

PACQUINO: But for so many? To succumb?

DAYTON: It requires conditions. Social disorder, general malaise. A time of radical re-ordering.

Pacquino eats it up.

DAYTON   (CONT'D): And then, starting with just a few... Shock troops. It helps if they are starving.

PACQUINO: Can do.

EXT. THE HORSESHOE CASINO - DAY

Surrounded by mock slot machines, a few enervated people lie prone on cots, fasting. A sign affixed to the wall: "Movement for Repentance". A couple dozen penitents parade around them.

Their signs read:

46

"God Does Not Play Dice!"
"Allaw of The Manifest!"
"No Machine Law!"

EXT. CITY HALL - DAY

Adherents to the "Movement for Repentance", picketing.

Their signs:
"Legislators Are NOT 'Like a Jury'"
"Baltimore For The Deserving!"
"Judges: Re-Try or Be Tried!"

EXT. STATE CAPITOL, ANNAPOLIS - DAY

Picketers from the Movement, some sling shotguns or rifles over their shoulders.

Their signs:
"Hands Off Our Ballots!"
"And... Our Bullets!"
"MD Constitution Says 'Elect!'"

EXT. DOWNTOWN BACK STREET – NIGHT

Bully boys beating up a man carrying a sign: "Support True Democracy! Support the People's Platform!" On the man's lapel, the green butterfly logo of the Confederates' Contingent

EXT. INNER HARBOR - DAY

In a light wind, Turk handles the tiller of a small rented sailboat, "The Brendan." Sylvia relaxes, enjoying the views.

TURK: Thanks for one more chance.

SYLVIA (indicating the sails): Interesting choice you've made, Melvin. A wind machine.

TURK: Melvin?

SYLVIA: I just thought... If we're going to try to work together, we need to be clear. Open.

TURK: OK, fine. But not Melvin. I mean... Well... Yeah, being open... exposing ourselves... that can be powerful.

SYLVIA: What do you mean? (suspicious) Exposing ourselves, powerful?

TURK (enthusiastic): Cliff Smith explained it. It's number twenty-two... Fully naked. Raw, sacrificial, innocent. Real. (impassioned) To expose one's body is to offer up one's soul.

SYLVIA (skeptical): Oh? I didn't realize you were religious.

Turk abruptly tacks the sailboat. Sylvia barely has time to duck under the boom.

TURK: Swinging around the other way, dealing with our current condition...

SYLVIA: Yes. Please do.

TURK: Secrecy. Cover up. Privacy. All the opposites of naked. Also necessary sometime. Protection from bribery, for instance.

SYLVIA: Please, Turk, what is it you...?

TURK: When people vote for public offices, as they used to here... the secret ballot is their protection against intimidation. But in the Platform, where we vote on policy matters openly...

SYLVIA: We're exposed.

TURK: Not only that. It means that some might be... easily... persuaded.

SYLVIA: Bribed? But, Turk, our salary is generous. A windfall for most.

TURK: Like I said. The old bunch. Still at it. Meat packers lugging heat, remember?

SYLVIA (cold): Too well.

TURK: Used to be simple for those guys. Campaign contributions.

SYLVIA: Some of that old bunch were my forebears. It might surprise you, but education early on, for some of us, meant we thrived.

TURK: Yeah, education. Lucky you.

SYLVIA: Why do you have to demean anything that doesn't fit your conception of economic correctness? (hesitates) Well-off, yes. My parents did manage to acquire reserves.

TURK (sneering): Never had to influence anybody? Lobbyist-free?

SYLVIA (determined): They tried to do the right thing. But politicians held important keys. Especially for us black folk. Since those politicians had to spend half their time looking for campaign support, I suppose...

TURK: Look, the fact is... You give a poor boy the time and money to study and deliberate... He... or she... can make better laws than any of those rich ones.

SYLVIA: Well, I didn't say you couldn't. What's most important about sortition is... Diversity of personalities. Not all of the same type, the type that can win elections.

Turk waits a moment, then leans to her ear and whispers.

TURK: I was approached. Sylvia doesn't hear, bends closer.

SYLVIA: A roach?

TURK: You? Into weed?

SYLVIA: Weeds? Oh, my garden? Yes, Clara convinced me to join one of the city's community gardens. As a way to show support for them. It's amazing to see what a transformation it is to get hands dirty. You should visit and...

TURK: Ah! Oh... (understanding her error) Look, a guy told me his foundation would make a substantial charitable donation to the arboretum, Clyburn. To bring the aquaponics to scale. Enough fish and fresh vegetables to feed all the food banks and homeless shelters. My folks would be part of it. They would love that.

SYLVIA: See! One of those... well-heeled meatpackers... doing the right thing.

TURK: Not exactly.

He hands her a glossy brochure about the Northwest Development Corporation at Pimlico.

EXT. COMMUNITY GARDEN – DAY'S LATER - DAY

Clara, in her wheelchair, peruses the brochure. Sylvia pulls weeds.

SYLVIA: All Turk has to do is to vote for a bill that sets up a Tax Increment Finance zone. A TIF. It's about a scheme to transform the Pimlico race track into a housing, retail and recreation area.

CLARA: Bribery, pure and simple. No longer disguised as campaign funding. (sarcastic) You think they might be more creative. A real estate deal...

SYLVIA: Dayton says it will transform the whole northwest sector.

CLARA: They're promoting it on TV. Hundreds of thousands for ads. TV, newspaper, social media. They're bribing the whole city.

SYLVIA: I was thinking... Since nobody's going to elect us based on our voting records...

CLARA: Yes?

SYLVIA: The only way they can know if their money talks is to see the individual votes taken in the Platform.

CLARA: Yes. So what?

SYLVIA: Why shouldn't we use the secret ballot? In the Platform.

CLARA: Hmm? That's novel.

SYLVIA: The secret vote to fight secret corruption.

CLARA: Progress, Sylvia. You're progressing. Your parents would be proud.

Sylvia fingers her crucifix.

SYLVIA: Whatever I thought when we were chosen... no longer matters. We're here now. Out of the blue. Anything we do, other than living up to the calling, would be... unfaithful.

INT./EXT. OFFICE BUILDING - DAY

Workers stumble, coughing, out of their cubicles. The fire alarm bell starts ringing. Workers make hasty exits from the building.

Some begin vomiting, some faint. In their deserted cubicles, computer screens are flashing.

ON COMPUTER SCREENS

"Suitcase nuclear device reported. Evacuation ordered."

INT. HEADQUARTERS FOR THE MOVEMENT FOR REPENTANCE - DAY

A clot of computer programmers, cackling. One pokes at her smart phone.

ON MANY SMART PHONES, A TWEET:

"Many sick radiation spreading"

INT. TELEVISION STUDIO

In the moments before going on air, the red LED counts down: 30, 29, 28, 27... The NEWSCASTER and the STATION DIRECTOR confer out of earshot of crew.

> NEWSCASTER: Reports are the cloud's moving west.

> STATION DIRECTOR: You know the protocol. Minimal info. Nothing false, just minimal. Prevent panic. Avoid contagion.

Under the desk, the newscaster surreptitiously taps into her smartphone: "FLEE!"

INT. "ACOLYTES OF ADAM" STOREFRONT CHURCH - NIGHT

Over the organ's rumble and behind a free-standing crucifix on a small altar, Preacher Alma Johnson whips up frenzy.

> PREACHER JOHNSON: And now the evil has descended upon the people in that building!

Shouts from the congregation of "Help Us, Lord!"

> PREACHER JOHNSON (CONT'D): I have seen the Black Hawk!

Placing her hands on the edge of the altar, she flips a hidden switch. The organist swells the bass. The crucifix starts jittering. She reaches for the Bible, closes her eyes, flings it open to a seemingly random page and reads.

>PREACHER JOHNSON (CONT'D): Job, Twenty-Seven. Verse Twenty-Two... Fleeeeee!

Congregants flee, off their rockers, into the streets.

EXT. "RUTH'S DINER" - DAY

Turk and Sanjit are pinned to the wall as the Acolytes of Adam rush past in a pack.

>Turk: Stampede!

>SANJIT: Hey, who shot the sheriff?

>TURK: Wild is free, how about it?

>SANJIT: How's anybody going to stop them, mon...? Before they trample everything?

INT. OFFICE OF MAYOR DAYTON - DAY

Jill Lasuli and Mayor Dayton palaver underneath a large portrait of a wreath-bedecked thoroughbred.

>LASULI: I want, like, assurances?

>DAYTON: You will get your pound of flesh, Miss Lasuli. (considers) Lasuli? Where's that name from? Central Asia, your people?

>LASULI: Maybe. What's it to you?

>DAYTON: Horseflesh. I've heard it's sweet?

LASULI: A real epicure.

DAYTON: Do you know how difficult this Movement is for my constituents? Out there on the streets, with the deranged? Our people want a Movement of Resistance. Not Repentance.

It seems his black skin turns blacker.

DAYTON (CONT'D): We've heard talk of militia. Crazy talk from secessionists in the hinterlands.

LASULI: So, you're in bed with Pacquino. So?

DAYTON: My people are out there holding their noses, alongside Pacquino's believers. (switching to snide) Oh, but... Dear Miss Lasuli, they are out there working for you-u-u.

LASULI: Ri-i-ight. And you're gonna, I mean, have them demanding protection for all that horse flesh at Pimlico, right?

DAYTON: Something like that, yes. But... Do I detect that the commission on a mere real estate deal may no longer be enough? Perhaps you prefer we should arrange something more... prestigious? Municipal Overseer of the Northwest Development Company?

Lasuli dispatches his lambast with silence.

DAYTON (CONT'D): So. This little Tweetie Bird's been doing some homework.

MONTAGE - THE RE-ZONING DEAL

-- On the streets of Park Heights neighborhood, near Pimlico: "Public Hearing: REZONING/#16-0653/Plat T-5-CO".

-- At the entrance to shuttered Pimlico, a sign designates: "Area Closed: Equine Quarantine"

-- Inside Pimlico, a barn placarded "Emerald Entity: At Auction."

>LASULI (O.S.): Just followed the money... Like they say? You're going to get your ducats. I know Shakespeare, too, smarty. When the TIF goes through.

BACK TO SCENE

>LASULI (CONT'D): Who cares if the plot just happens to be, like, next to the projected prime retail space? Recently purchased? By a certain major donor? Of yours? Not that it'll, I mean, increase the value or anything.

>DAYTON: Well espied, Ms. Louche Lasuli. I thought you might appreciate the quarantine. A little pixie dust for Iris Reid. We must take care. Prying eyes in the Platform. Not to mention the media.

>LASULI: Seems to me that most of the media's sight is over The Movement? Over your friend, the reverend's Movement?

DAYTON: Yes, but snoops are everywhere. The police can't always be diverted. And there are those busybodies on the Platform. They've got a Select Committee on Oversight.

LASULI: The Movement's, like, succeeding, right? Like a good bowel movement?

DAYTON: Please. Indeed... Miss Louche. (mock lament) What can the poor People's Platform do? Up against penitents the good reverend has on their knees.

INT. "CONFEDERATES' CONTINGENT" OFFICE - DAY

Turk, Sylvia, Sanjit and Clara sit with The Organizer, eyes glued to an official 1922 Fascist silent film.

ON PROJECTION SCREEN -- "MUSSOLINI MARCHES ON ROME"

THE ORGANIZER (O.S.): It's not as far-fetched as you might think. Mussolini's march on Rome was much smaller than King's on Washington. But Mussolini's forces took power. They had generated a climate of fear.

The projected silent movie ends.

THE ORGANIZER (CONT'D): Granted, Baltimore is only a city, not a national capital. But we're an incubator. The big boys and girls down in D-C, they aren't dummies.

CLARA: They ought to be quaking. If sortition succeeds here... And shows the nation what a real democracy can be. (almost gloating) Coming to next to the General Assembly... And then to the Capitol. Soon!

They all give Clara a little silent handclap.

TURK: So what to do now?

THE ORGANIZER: Make friends. Offer to support whatever harmless cockamamie idea potential allies may spout.

TURK: Man, you blowing smoke?

THE ORGANIZER: Look here, bro'... The only solution to any shortcoming of democracy is... more democracy. Get organized.

SYLVIA: I think we should hold a prayer service with The Movement. An offer to reconcile.

THE ORGANIZER (eyes roll): They're beyond the pale.

SYLVIA (prissy): No one is beyond the pale.

THE ORGANIZER: Look, the Maryland Court of Appeal's decision seemed to close the debate. But now, in come politics and piety. (flustered) Damn! And you want to...

A rock crashes through the window. The Organizer rushes to the window to see a man, his face concealed by an orange bandana, running away.

Turk and Sanjit run outside but the rock thrower has disappeared. The Confederates' Contingent's placard is defaced with a strike-through: "The CON~~FEDERATES'~~ CON~~TINGENT~~."

EXT. SUBURBAN MANSION - DAYS LATER - DAY

The home of Reverend Pacquino, besieged by news media. He faces microphones.

>PACQUINO: We deplore the incidents of violence. Our people do not want escalation. But terrorists threaten. We direct our followers to pray. To continue to pray. To restore democracy to our beloved city.

INSERT - HEADLINES OF CONFUSION

-- Newspaper: *"Baltimore Sun:* New Followers Resist Repentance of the Old Guard"

-- Internet: "*Baltimore Beat:* Nix to General Strike"

-- Magazine: "*Baltimore Afro-American:* "Sneak Peek: The Rev Revs Up!"

-- Tweet: "*WYPR:* Repentance Relents"

INT. OFFICE OF MAYOR DAYTON - DAY

Dayton and Lasuli share cheese, crackers and wine under the portrait of that prize-winning racehorse.

>LASULI: Mayor, like, before fate brought us together, I always thought you were The Best! The way you delivered. Pulled the strings? What now, with The Movement?

DAYTON: A diversionary tactic, my dear. The price of re-election. I must mouth religious claptrap now and again. (solicitous) But I feel for the non-believers among my supporters. Out there with their earnest slogans and picket signs. Love the dupes.

LASULI: Dupes?

DAYTON: Sorry. Your "louche" tends to get in the way. It's one thing for you... to be disreputable and appealing. I don't have the luxury.

LASULI: How d'ya figure?

DAYTON: Too many Fourth of July parades, waving my fool head off at the masses. Voters don't do louche. They only do appealing.

LASULI: Wow, a lesson I should learn? Next time I, like, walk in a parade?

DAYTON: Strut a catwalk, more likely.

LASULI: What happens if The Movement collapses? What'll you do for your... dupes?

DAYTON: I'll have to compensate them. Box seats to a game of their choosing. A little something to cover up their errors. (self-deprecating) Pitiful.

LASULI: And for the ones on their knees?

DAYTON: Oh, Pacquino will figure out something. Prophets fail all the time. Their stock in trade. Decay, then resurrection. Endlessly fascinating, that.

LASULI: What about that poor-boy, the reformed psycho? With a pole up his ass. And the other one? The Princess, like... guarded by The Crip'?

DAYTON: They are reachable. Every... body... is reachable.

LASULI: Every body is, like, a dupe?

DAYTON: Every body has eyes for some kind of splash. You just watch. Those two are nature lovers. They will want to investigate something. About the Arboretum or the Conservatory. Or... the tulip park in Homeland. Some "issue."

LASULI: Well, they are legislators, aren't they? By, for and of...?

DAYTON: Pah! By The People, my ass. (apprising) And yours.

LASULI: Choice, Mayor. I mean, like, yeah, my grandaddies, the Huns.

Lasuli looks up to the portrait of the racehorse.

LASULI (CONT'D): Choice cuts?

EXT. "EMERALD ENTITY" BUILDING AT PIMLICO - DAY

Three "HANDS" trim horses' hooves.

CHAWING "HAND": I seen a TV show on it. It warn't no hoax. T'was a test. Them terrorists... they run fakes all the time. Lookin' for weak spots.

SMOKING "HAND": Guv'ment'll hide that... Don't want us to know. Hell, don't make no difference t' me.

CHAWING "HAND": Sure did panic 'em. City folk, scared 'a their own shadows. Jes' thought of a dirty bomb had 'em on their knees.

SMOKING "HAND": What you think'a DAYTON:? He's been in the seat for a while.

CHAWING "HAND": Too long. Can't trust 'em when they been there long.

SMOKING "HAND": That reverend's okay.

SPITTING "HAND": Never thought I'd join nothin'.

CHAWING "HAND": We ain't fastin', at least.

SMOKING "HAND": Jes' gotta keep the lassoes limber. In case. Fer a little persuadin'.

CHAWING "HAND": Best persuadin'd be ta shoot one of them judges. Switch that vote the other way. Three-to-four. That'd do it sure.

INT. LABORATORY, FORT DETRICK, MARYLAND - DAY

In full biohazard suit, Pacquino's advisor Crisanto enters a room marked "BioSafety Level 4". He drains the liquid from a beaker into a flask labeled "Infectious Substance, Category A, Affecting Humans." He places the flask into an unmarked aluminum box.

Crisanto closes the box and locks it with a key. He takes it with him, out of the high-security environment, into his office where he deposits the box into a file cabinet.

INT. "THE CHARLES" MOVIE THEATER – NIGHT

Turk and Sanjit watch the last scene of "Treasure of the Sierra Madre". Two gold miners belly-laugh about the gold dust they have struggled for, blowing away in the wind. Movie ends. Turk and Sanjit exit.

SANJIT: What it is, mon. Always, no matter. What it comes down to in the end.

Jill Lasuli appears out of nowhere and stops them in their tracks.

LASULI: Representative Polat? What a coincidence! I'm staff director for Iris Reid, from Ohio?

Turk shakes her hand. Sanjit does as well.

SANJIT: We occupy the same position, m'am.

LASULI (sassy): I was hoping you'd say that.

Turk squints at Sanjit, wondering.

LASULI (CONT'D): Got some time? We might, like, have a little something in common.

The three enter a neighborhood bar.

INT. CHAMBER OF THE PEOPLE'S PLATFORM - DAY

The Chair gavels the session closed. Lots of glad-handing among Turk, Sylvia, Cliff Smith, Iris Reid and Jas Robinson.

TURK (to Cliff Smith): Yeah, man. Sure. Hang gliders, not drones. Make the munition makers uncomfortable. You'll have my vote.

CLIFF SMITH: Ecstasy, not entropy. Rapture, not rapacity. Northrop Grumman has to re-tool.

SYLVIA: We agree. (to Jas Robinson): And a start towards a higher minimum wage has to be made. (to Iris Reid): Thank you for your help with the votes.

IRIS REID (to Turk): We had to twist a few arms. My staff director is good at that. We got it done.

The Chair of the People's Platform ambles over. Turk and Sylvia meet him.

THE CHAIR: Impressive, the way you mustered support for the rule change.

SYLVIA: Thank you for expediting it. Secret voting will protect against corruption.

Turk starts to give an enthusiastic thumbs-up but, realizing its impropriety, quickly drops it.

Platform Member Antonia Baldwin pops in, smirks at Turk.

ANTONIA BALDWIN: (to The Chair): So much for a new day of transparency. Goodbye to any Sunshine Ordinance. (head shaking) The people are going to kill us.

THE CHAIR: I don't think so, Ms. Baldwin. The secret vote will demonstrate how serious this Platform is when it comes to resisting special interests.

Baldwin stomps away.

INT. DEAD END STREET - NIGHT

Outside the fence on the backside of Mount Olivet Cemetery, Lasuli and Dayton sit in two separate cars, cop-sex alignment: next to and facing each other, windows down.

> LASULI: Okay, like, we're here. Like a drop spot in *The Wire.* Satisfied?

> DAYTON (droll): I always wanted to be in the movies.

> LASULI: So, congratulations. Ya ever seen that old flick, about the guy that Goes-to-Washington?

Dayton has.

> LASULI (CONT'D): It's, like, a take-off of that one.

Dayton's quizzical glance doesn't interrupt her.

> LASULI (CONT'D): She swallowed it. (flicking her tongue) Like, whole? She got her committee, Housing and Urban Affairs, to approve the TIF. For Northwest Development? It's buried, like, in the omnibus bill?

> DAYTON: Impressive, how she persuaded colleagues about the rule change.

> LASULI: Yeah, we even got that air head, the Anatolian Wrestler...? Iris, like, traded...? Her support for the secret vote for his on the omnibus. (crass irony) Like, wow, wheeler-dealers, hunh?

Dayton hands Lasuli a briefcase.

DAYTON: A little extra credit.

Lasuli takes a quick look, plenty of hundred dollar bills.

LASULI: Gee, Mayor. All for, like, little ole disreputably appealing... me?

Dayton winks and hands her a copy of the *Baltimore Sun*. Its headline reads: "Rebellion Simmers"

INT. "RUTH'S DINER" - DAY

Turk, Sanjit, Ruth and Tom Moore looking at the television monitor up high and behind the counter.

ON TELEVISION - ROUGH STUFF

Hooligans beating up shoppers trying to enter a supermarket.

TV REPORTER (V.O.): Incidents of violence continue to plague factions of The Movement for Repentance. Nonetheless, The Movement seems to have stalled.

BACK TO SCENE

Turk and Sanjit high-five.

RUTH: Careful, don't get slap happy.

TURK (miasmic): My mind glides through a labyrinth.

TOM MOORE: Your mind-glide is no protection against firearms. The other side, they don't play.

ON TELEVISION – EXT. BALTIMORE'S FOUR
SEASONS HOTEL - DAY

A live feed captioned "Breaking News: Circling the
Wagons".

Limousines disgorge well-dressed men and women. In the
background, a street billboard: "The People's CON! Secret
Vote = Secret Theft -- Paid for by Recover Our City"

>TV REPORTER: Financial supporters for The
>Movement for Repentance are gathering here for a
>closed-door conclave. As you see behind me, they
>have created Recover-Our-City. Earlier in the day
>we spoke with the Movement's leader, the
>Reverend Emmanuel Pacquino.

ON TELEVISION – EXT. PACQUINO'S SUBURBAN
MANSION - DAY

Pacquino stands at the open front door with several
microphones aimed at him.

>TV REPORTER: It seems, Reverend, that you are
>losing control of some elements in your Movement.
>Isn't it true that nonviolent campaigns often
>disintegrate and are taken over by others? These
>reports of violence...

>PACQUINO: Our penitents continue their fasts.
>Some newcomers fail to understand our intentions.

>TV REPORTER: What is behind rumors about a
>so-called Orange Faction?

>PACQUINO: Some are losing patience. Is that any
>surprise? *Tsch!* (catching himself) But that's
>enough. (soldierly) We-Will-Be-The-One!

He retreats, slamming shut the door.

EXT. THE JONES FALL TRAIL - DAY

Turk and Sylvia bicycle past Mayor Dayton, on foot. Sylvia takes the initiative to circle back. Turk follows. They dismount.

> SYLVIA: Hello, Mayor. Do you come out here often?

> DAYTON: Yes, I like to walk. Clears out the mind's detritus.

> SYLVIA: Gardening does it for me.

> TURK (stand-offish): Bicycling. The wind.

> SYLVIA: Hands dirty, you know?

> DAYTON: Hands dirty?

> SYLVIA: Not really. Dirt is just dirt. And compost is clean.

> DAYTON: I can't abide the smell.

> TURK (dander up): You think it's... excrement? Feces?

> DAYTON (even-keeled): On investigations abroad I've seen cesspools used for fertilizer. And...

> TURK: The stink of shit is just a strong smell.

> DAYTON: If you say so.

> SYLVIA (mediating): Properly assembled compost piles are not odiferous.

DAYTON: Thank you, madam. I'm gun-shy when talk turns to corruption. That's what we are talking about, isn't it? Rot.

SYLVIA: Maybe you'd agree that, if the end result is clean, what matter the source?

DAYTON: A pragmatist. I would never have expected...

SYLVIA: You may call it pragmatic, Mayor. I rather call it nature's sublimity. In religious terms, grace.

DAYTON: Well, it's a beautiful DAY
 for a walk. Might say it's alchemical.

TURK (still cranky): Now you're talking, Mayor. Even the old guard can morph...

Dayton chuckles, takes a look at Turk's bicycle.

DAYTON: Nice bike. Would you say it represents... a transformation of decay? Metallurgical?

Turk starts at the unexpected comment.

TURK (blurts): When the mind glides, there comes a rush, a cataract.

DAYTON: Hmm? A cataract?
TURK: Yeah... and its lifting.

Dayton cogitates, eyes lifted to the puffy white clouds. Then he flicks open his fist, acknowledging the double entendre. Smiles, chuckles more, walks on.

INT. "THE BARBARIAN" SPORTS BAR - DAYS LATER - DAY

Dayton and his Intern nurse libations. Dayton points to "The Dying Gaul" replica.

> DAYTON (O.S.): Jefferson wanted the original at Monticello.

> INTERN: When you bring Reverend Pacquino in here, isn't he offended?

> DAYTON: I rather like to see him squirm.

Dayton still gazes at the statue.

> DAYTON (CONT'D): The Gauls, Celts in Anatolia, faced heavily armored troops... naked. The Greeks reported it to be a terrifying spectacle. (chuckling) Our poor Reverend.

INT. "ACOLYTES OF ADAM" STOREFRONT CHURCH - DAY

Preacher Johnson peers down from the pulpit, listening to her congregation respond to a question she has posed.

> RUDDY CONGREGANT: Maybe it's true.

> PALE CONGREGANT: The crucifix moved. That was true.

> DUSKY CONGREGANT: But the dirty bomb was a hoax.

> PREACHER JOHNSON: Let us pray.

70

The organist hits the low bass and Johnson secretly switches the button for infrasound. Wailing and trembling commence.

Reverend Pacquino bounds in. And shivers. The organist stops and Johnson secretly switches off the infrasound.

> PACQUINO: You stayed true. Your faith was tested. But you believed! The Movement... The Movement for Repentance. Survives!

The congregants shake themselves free of their fright.

> PALE CONGREGANT: The crucifix moved! I saw it. We all did.

> PACQUINO: At Allways my congregation saw spirits. Some heard The Word.

> PREACHER JOHNSON: Reverend, these are strange times. Spirits manifesting. Fake bombs. Some say the city is about to split to pieces. The Black Hawk is flying.

> PACQUINO (sharply, contradicting): The *anito,* as we call them in the country of my birth... Angels. *Salamat!* Thank you, thank you Lord! ...that so many believe in angels!

> PREACHER JOHNSON (complying): Yes. We thank you and the *anito* at Allways Church of the Salvation. For your spiritual support and for your financial donations.

> PACQUINO (vaguely threatening): At Allways, we tithe. Our bounty is for you, our brethren. Who believe.

Preacher Johnson raises her hands to praise the Lord and signals the choir to break into jubilation.

EXT. MOUNTAINTOP, WESTERN MARYLAND - DAY

A bright clear August day. Sanjit watches Turk strap himself into a hang glider displaying the logo of a rental outfit.

> TURK: This recess thing is freaking okay. Ah, if papa could see his little Turkey take off now.

> SANJIT: Ah, I tell you, mon... always wanted to come out west. As kids we loved the westerns. Tried to learn rope tricks.

> TURK: Let's just hope I don't drift into West Virginia. Into the midst of some heat-packing Open Carriers. They might take a mind to shoot... (laughing) A high flyer from the bad old Baltimore.

> SANJIT: Somebody out here did say, a local pol... he was going to protect the tradition... of turkey shoots.

Turk shoots an eye at his staff director. Who winks.

> SANJIT (CONT'D) (more seriously): He actually said that three states might be better than one. The secessionist...

> TURK: Let him say what he likes. It's a free country. We've still got the People's Con... Contingent... if we need them.

> SANJIT: OK, bossman... Time now you take the lay of the land.

Turk leaps off the mountain.

TURK: In air we trust!

INT. FOREST PARK BRANCH LIBRARY READING ROOM - DAY

Back near her neighborhood, Sylvia browses the magazine rack. She notices Dayton's face on a cover.

One headline reads: "Corruption in the Hall". Another: "Underground Resistance Spreads."

She flips to the first article.

INSERT - ARTICLE "CORRUPTION IN THE HALL"

-- Photo of Jill Lasuli under arrest, escorted by a deputy sheriff. Caption: "Platform staffer accused of real estate scam."

-- Photo of Mayor Dayton giving a news conference in front of the "Emerald Entity" building at Pimlico. A large sign behind him: "Democracy = Electoral Choice." Caption: "Dayton repeats demand for the law's repeal."

-- Photo of the assembled People's Platform. Caption: "Dayton says 'Secret vote protected accused.'"

Sylvia turns the page to the other story.

INSERT - HEADLINE: "UNDERGROUND RESISTANCE SPREADS"

-- Photo of a ragtag bunch of toughs in bizarre orange camouflage, brandishing rifles and mortars. Caption: "Militia calls itself 'The Orange Array'"

-- Photo of a map of Maryland broken into three pieces: east, west and central. Caption: "Group promotes partition."

EXT. WAR MEMORIAL PLAZA - DAY

Early September, lunchtime at the green space in front of City Hall. Sylvia and Clara open their wicker basket. Turk and Sanjit take out water bottles from their backpacks. Picnic on the lawn.

> CLARA: Only the un-elected can make the tough, long-term decisions required for the greater good.

> SANJIT: We should tackle the big urban issues. Like... Breaking the defacto redlining that maintains impoverished ghettos. Like... Improving public transport. Like... Urban farms, not food deserts. Like... Aquaponics, micro-loans, cooperative housing projects.

The other three are all ears.

> SANJIT (CONT'D): We can get travel expenses for some research. Check out innovations in other cities. We can make a difference.

> TURK: And since we're on a roll... Why do we need an elected mayor?

> SANJIT: You want to take on everything?

> TURK: Mayoral candidates could present themselves to the Platform. We elect one and be done with it.

> CLARA: The end of interminable electioneering.

SANJIT (laughing): Fiscal conservatives will have to love it!

CLARA: Possible. Who knows what's to come?

Turk removes a bright green whirligig-butterfly from his backpack and gives it to Sylvia.

SYLVIA (smiling, to Clara): Surprises. Only surprises.

INT. CHAMBER OF THE PEOPLE'S PLATFORM - DAY

The Chair presides over one-minute speeches. Platform Member Jas Robinson stands unsteady at a podium.

JAS ROBINSON: Madam Chair... The thing I want to say is... It seems like we're always talking about growing. The Bible says: There is a time for everything. Maybe this is a time when some ought to stand still. Let those behind catch up.

LATER

Platform Member Antonia Baldwin, self-assured as always, reading from a book.

ANTONIA BALDWIN: That government is best which governs not at all; and when men are prepared for it, that will be the kind of government which they will have. (puts the book down) Henry David Thoreau.

LATER

Platform Member Iris Reid, schoolmarmish.

IRIS REID: Some say that the People's Platform is as prone to abandon its principles as every other group of reformers who got a taste of power. I want the record to show that my staff director is not one of those...

LATER

Platform Member Cliff Smith, declaiming.

CLIFF SMITH: Munition makers twist minds into killing machines. There are whole nations that live without armies. Here in the city, what we need is a police force that makes nonviolent means its priority.

INT. CITY HALL CORRIDOR – LATER

Dayton bumps into Lasuli. Lasuli ignores his companion.

LASULI: Some of these yokels in there were, like, born for lambast? Don'cha think?

DAYTON: They provide pleasant diversions.

LASULI: I hear militias are forming in the western counties. In the mountains. They're issuing death threats. Not exactly pleasant diversions.

DAYTON: Oh, a little *fatwa* from our more enthusiastic patriots shouldn't be taken too seriously. Remember what that old Virginian slave master recommended the new republic: A little blood should be spilled every few years. To water the tree of liberty.

LASULI: Yeah, well... I'm, like, out on bond? My own blood spilled. Like, thank you?

DAYTON: A small price. A pin prick. And taken care of.

LASULI: You owe me. The public's not exactly happy about secret voting in the Platform. They want, you know, blood sport? The tabloids are bored with this representation... proportional-to-the-willing-and-the- able. (tongue out) Lame! (switching to seductive) Besides, poo-poo-pee-do, we were supposed to be creating a... diversion? Seems everything now is, like... more, unh, inscrutable... than diverting?

DAYTON: Inscrutable can be diverting.

INT. NORTHROP GRUMMAN, LINTHICUM, MARYLAND - DAY

In a factory room bannered with "C4ISR," robotics assemble electronic communication components on an assembly line.

WORKERS, all female, pass flyers around:
"Don't Tread On Us!"
"Take Back Our State Constitution!"
"#1 Now and Forever!"
"Award Those Who Can!"

GRUFF WORKER: Talk's cheap. I ain't no protestor.

ROTUND WORKER: One of them representatives, she says she believes in the-flow-of-water. Says it's The Way. Can you beat that?

SQUEAMISH WORKER: This stuff we're building... C-Four-I-S-R... Command, Control, Communications, Computers, Intelligence, Surveillance and Reconnaissance...whew! (gazing around factory) Good enough to fight foreigners but... Hate to use it to fight each other.

EXT. 32ND STREET FARMERS MARKET - DAY

Amidst the bounty of harvest time, vendors and farmers look suspiciously at the same flyers.

LEATHERY FARMER: Three-way split up? Okay by me.

TIRED FARMER: What's the difference? They all gotta eat.

HOBBLING FARMER: We'd get along just fine.

INT. SHOE STORE - DAY

The SALESMAN hands flyers to the STORE MANAGER.

SALESMAN: I hear they're talking about secession in the western counties. Maybe the eastern shore, too.

STORE MANAGER: How would that help us?

SALESMAN: I don't know but...

STORE MANAGER: And just who is going to take on City Hall? Much less, Annapolis? You think some body's just going to be able to walk in and...

SALESMAN: Yeah. The Orange Array.

INT. OFFICE OF "ALLWAYS" CHURCH - DAY

Reverend Pacquino and Crisanto strategize.

> PACQUINO: In my country it was not what you could do that mattered. But who you knew. In this People's Platform, so-called, it matters not who you know. *Tsch!*

> CRISANTO: Once the grandstanders finish blowing off steam, it will degrade into Go-along-to-get-along. None will dare excel.

> PACQUINO: We already hear it. They talk about standing still. Stopping economic growth. *Tsch!* They would abandon the cornucopia. Given by The Manifest. For all we need. And all we want!

EXT. INNER HARBOR - DAYS LATER - DAY

Dayton, Pacquino and Lasuli stand on the after deck of the super-yacht "Firefly" as its captain guides the boat through the harbor.

> DAYTON: ... and you thought we'd lost our access when they went to the secret vote?

> PACQUINO: How do you say? A pig's ear...?

> DAYTON: A sow's ear into... in this case, a winning purse. Yes, that's it. And on top of that, trying to eliminate me!

> PACQUINO: To elect the mayor. Themselves!

DAYTON: Loved that proposal: to wait for those behind to catch up. A plea for economic contraction. Push even more businesses out of the city! Could we have asked for more?

LASULI: Enough gloating, Mayor. Ain't it, like, time? I'm supposed to reap what you sowed? You got your TIF. Our deal? The fruit, remember? I'm hungry.

Dayton nods dismissively.

INT. SYLVIA'S APARTMENT - CONTINUOUS

The whole room is shaking. A small potted plant falls off the shelf. Church bells are ringing. The building's fire alarm blares. Sylvia and Clara, terrified.

CLARA: Earthquake!

EXT. INNER HARBOR - CONTINUOUS

On the yacht, it's flat water, no indication of earthquake.

DAYTON (to Lasuli): Enjoyed your jail time, did you?

Lasuli steps closer, threatening.

LASULI: I can like expose you, y'know!

PACQUINO steps between them, but adds fuel...

PACQUINO: I can expose you both.

DAYTON: You're as exposed as we are, Reverend... Apocalypse... of the Infrasound.

Guiterrez steps back a step, on guard.

DAYTON (CONT'D): Naked. The three of us. All bare. Tempting, Reverend? Fight it out in the buff?

Pacquino gags, shuddering at the thought. He points his finger like an imaginary pistol at DAYTON:.

PACQUINO: You are? You would? (unaware of implication): Em-Bare-Ass me... *Tsch!*

LASULI: Not so fast, Apocalypse!

PACQUINO: What I do for The Manifest is necessary. The people need help to believe. Infrasound...

Lasuli draws her own imaginary finger gun, pointing at Pacquino.

LASULI: Enough with your hypocrisy.

Dayton pulls out his index finger, aiming at Lasuli.

DAYTON: And enough, little lady... of protecting your sweet little rump.

The three are frozen in Mexican stand-off. Pacquino aimed at Dayton; Dayton aimed at Lasuli; Lasuli aimed at Pacquino.

DAYTON (CONT'D) (calculating): I shoot first, Louche goes down. But Apocalypse gets me...

EXT. SYLVIA'S APARTMENT BUILDING - CONTINUOUS

Sylvia and Clara emerge from the building. The earthquake has subsided. A CROWD mills around, disoriented. Some are looking at, or speaking into, their smart phones.

VOICES FROM THE CROWD: Earthquake? Here? / Is it safe now? / Aftershocks are weaker. / Usually. / Huge damage in the Midwest! / The Midwest? / It's The Big One, New Madrid. Richter Seven-Point-Nine!

EXT. INNER HARBOR - CONTINUOUS

On the yacht, the three collaborators eyeball each other, stuck in showdown.

> DAYTON (magnanimous): But who wants to argue philosophy?

Slowly, they re-holster their imaginary weapons.

> LASULI (conciliatory): Yeah, yeah. Like, that's my point.

> PACQUINO: Infection. Philosophy is infection.

> DAYTON: True, true... What difference does philosophy make to the atmospheric static of a random number generator?

The small rented sailboat "Brendan" approaches. Sanjit at the tiller, Turk at the bow.

> SANJIT: Hail! Hail! And a hearty Ho!

> TURK: The People's Navy on patrol!

Turk holds up his smart phone. And taps his temple.

> DAYTON (to the captain): All Ahead! Buster!

> TURK (shouting): We just have been informed...

82

The captain guns the throttle, drowning him out. As it speeds away the yacht's wake nearly swamps the sailboat.

> PACQUINO: Oh, so many have lost faith. They forget what ancestors fought for. They throw themselves to the wind.

> DAYTON (ironic): That's the way they are. Unguided. Emotionally profligate. (pure snark) Intellectually doctrinaire.

Dayton notices people on shore running amok.

> DAYTON (CONT'D): Slower, Captain!

He picks up binoculars and scans.

> PACQUINO: What is it?

> DAYTON: Looks like an emergency.

EXT. SYLVIA'S APARTMENT BUILDING - CONTINUOUS

> CLARA (to Sylvia): We're over seven hundred miles from the epicenter!

EXT. INNER HARBOR - LATER

> LASULI: , Dayton and Pacquino walk to their automobiles in a parking lot. No signs of any earthquake damage.

> DAYTON: Now, now, children, let us not...

> PACQUINO: You think this... just... happened? The Manifest does not just happen. The Manifest sends us... a sign!

83

Lasuli hides her face, desperately trying not to explode.

> DAYTON (playing sagacious): I recall an aphorism... We will always exist in one form or another. (fingers the wind) Where did that come from?

> GUTIERREZ: The Manifest.

> LASULI: Quantum physics.

> DAYTON: A jolly threesome, we. Not one spear point, but a trident.

EXT. DOCK ON INNER HARBOR - CONTINUOUS

Turk and Sanjit disembark from their sailboat. Turk is on his phone.

> TURK: You're okay, Sylvia? (listens) Yes, Sanjit and I were on the water. Didn't feel a thing... (listens) Right, I checked it on the phone.

INT. OFFICE OF "ALLWAYS" MEGACHURCH - DAY

Surrounded by advisors including Crisanto and Bayani, Reverend Pacquino screams into his phone.

> PACQUINO: The Manifest! Manifesting! The quake. The believers know. It is The Movement! The very earth... (stops to listen, then..) No! No, Johnson! It is not the time! Not about the angels! Not your Black Hawk. Not your madonna! But about The Movement!

He angrily snaps off the phone, tossing it on his desk.

PACQUINO (CONT'D): That woman. Those people! *Tsch!* One story at a time. All they can handle. Angels or devils. Not both. *Tsch!* If I cut off their dole, they'd straighten up.

CRISANTO: How about ratcheting up our megaphone, so to speak?

Distracted, Pacquino signals he'll entertain the intrusion.

CRISANTO (CONT'D): We should post, on the doors of the Platform... Demands! Theses!

PACQUINO: What? I do a Martin Luther?

BAYANI: We can't trust Dayton and his crowd. They aren't believers. We should march on City Hall!

PACQUINO: Oh, a Martin Luther King?

CRISANTO: A little of each. Wouldn't hurt.

PACQUINO: Not aimed at the pope, but at... ?

CRISANTO: At the inaccessible, the unaccountable, the conspiratorial, so-called deliberators... The Un-Elected!

Pacquino likes it, smiles, nodding agreement.

PACQUINO: Ah, a march. But not like King. Not to beg. But to take over. To reign.

BAYANI: What, by the way, should be our response to that radio journalist? Our encouragement of fecundity...

CRISANTO: He asked if we were like the Nazis, the Orthodox Jews and the Palestinian nationalists.

PACQUINO: A joker, hey? Ah, let them worry. That we will dominate. Out-breed them... (salaciously triumphant) We will. We-Will-Be-The-Ones!

Hearty laughter all around.

INT. "RUTH'S DINER" - DAY

With the place nearly empty Ruth is free to talk with Sanjit as he eats breakfast at the counter. Television coverage of the earthquake.

RUTH: Two hundred years since the last big Midwest quake. And, terrible as it is for those folks, I can't help being fascinated. Why is that?

SANJIT: It's the bad bounce, Ruthie. The random event. An error! We're addicted to the extraordinary.

EXT. INNER HARBOR - DAY

Dayton and Pacquino walk along the wharf.

DAYTON: So, Reverend, how far are you willing to go?

PACQUINO: You refer to?

DAYTON: Friends of mine at Fort Detrick tell me that a determined solitary individual, with access to certain nerve agents, could deploy a weapon of mass destruction... alone.

PACQUINO: You see! It takes only a few. The Array, your people and mine. A small group, focused. We-Will-Be-The-One!

DAYTON: Problem with bioweapons is that the stuff is alive. Once released it continues to spread. My contacts say a lone individual could engineer one that had no antidote.

PACQUINO: The Manifest uses All Means. Those who believe Allaw... They will survive. A new Passover. For the others... (darkly) Many are called...

Dayton turns to the *U.S.S. Constellation*.

DAYTON: Your lifeboat, then, Reverend? Too small for all of us?

A Coast Guard helicopter passes over.

DAYTON (CONT'D): Our military, egalitarian and meritocratic. You'd be willing, Reverend, to bring everything down?

PACQUINO: Too many question authority. They fail to recognize author-ship. Fail to recognize Allaw. The Word of The Manifest.

DAYTON (admonishing): Those who strive for supremacy, reverend, must balance the safety of belief with the uncertainty that comes with the search for knowledge.

PACQUINO: You think so, Mayor? You think so?

An eagle gyres above the CSX railroad yards at Curtis Bay.

EXT. CURTIS BAY - CONTINUOUS

A tremendous explosion blows apart a tank car marked "Inhalation Hazard -- Chlorine." Green gas floats slowly across the Patapsco River towards Sparrow Point.

EXT. COMMUNITY GARDEN - SAME TIME

Sylvia tends her plot, harvesting squash. Clara rakes up the autumn's debris. Turk's whirligig spins gaily.

The sound of the railroad explosion has startled them.

> SYLVIA: That was a loud one.

> CLARA: They must be demolishing something. Before construction, destruction...

> SYLVIA: Think we should plant kale? Will it overwinter, you think?

> CLARA: It's a little late.

> SYLVIA: Buy some starts from the garden center.

Clara nods "good idea."

> CLARA: I'm glad you convinced me to join you here.

> SYLVIA: I couldn't face another barrage of questioning.

> CLARA: Funny, what that one reporter brought up. About the long-term threats. That it isn't weapons?

> SYLVIA: True. The plow has devastated more land than ever the sword did.

SYLVIA (CONT'D) (pondering): If someone could breed a perennial grain, we could end tillage and most irrigation.

CLARA: Genetic modification?

SYLVIA: Maybe. I read the research. They're looking for beneficial inherited traits. Outliers. The random 'sports.'

EXT. INNER HARBOR - SAME DAY

Bird's eye view of the Patapsco River. A thin stream of chlorine gas pours from the damaged rail car. It drifts slowly southeast down the middle of the river, away from habitations.

Pacquino and Dayton walk fast toward the parking lot.

DAYTON (angry): What is it with your people? Inbred sociopaths? Loose cannons? We said we wouldn't hit first.

PACQUINO: No. I didn't authorize...

DAYTON: Rogues?

PACQUINO: Many are called...

DAYTON: Oh, please. Just shut up.

INT. OFFICE OF IRIS REID - DAYS LATER - DAY

Iris Reid fidgets at her desk, entranced and entrapped by her staff director, Lasuli.

LASULI: Yeah, yeah, the governor's decree... counts. State of emergency. But, like, you gotta get the people to obey? Y'know? Without that, the mayor... and the whole friggin' thing has, like, no clothes? Get it?

IRIS REID: I suppose... I was wondering...

LASULI: Look, I mean, we've got the storefront people convinced that the earthquake was, like, caused by infrasound?

IRIS REID: And...?

LASULI: Well, that means that a whole lot more "believers"... From all over the state...? They'll join the bandwagon.

IRIS REID: Oh. Unh, why?

LASULI: It's a counterfactual. Obvious? You know how hard it is, like, to get people to believe stuff? I mean, stuff that hasn't happened?

IRIS REID: Oh, ah, yes... I see.

LASULI: Truth is, the people don't need, I mean, to understand. All they need is a body? To follow. One that appears strong... (puffing up) Forthright, clear and, like... able to deliver? Someone like... Not to worry! Like...

She makes the sound of a horn.

LASULI (CONT'D) (BLAAATT!) You...

She pounds the table, doubling with laughter.

LASULI (CONT'D): Not!

INT. "ACOLYTES OF ADAM" STOREFRONT CHURCH - DAY

Reverend Pacquino and Preacher Johnson are in the middle of a heated argument. Parishioners surround them, listening in.

>PACQUINO (declaiming): *Tsch*! I said The Manifest works in wondrous ways! *Tsch!*

>PREACHER JOHNSON (accusatory): I thought you believed in miracles, Reverend?

>PACQUINO: Your mumbo-jumbo -- Madonna and Hawk -- didn't blow that chlorine away from the city.

>PREACHER JOHNSON: So it isn't always a matter of tricks? Your boys just forgot to look at the weather report?

>PACQUINO (getting hotter): How The Manifest creates miracles is not up to us. We are tools. We make the miracle. The time is now! Into the streets!

>PREACHER JOHNSON (insinuating): Other kinds of tricks, Reverend! Some you may remember. Ones my father told. Ones that only a woman can turn.

Pacquino backs a half step. Where's Johnson going with this?

>PREACHER JOHNSON (CONT'D): You said our Movement's failure showed the futility of striking head on. Was it your mother, Reverend, who showed you something... Something else about that?

PACQUINO: What? Didn't I tell you to just... Insert
- young Pacquino's memory

Several quick scenes of the boy Pacquino witnessing his
naked mother fucking a series of U.S. sailors.

PACQUINO (O.S.): ... keep... your... mouth... shut!

BACK TO SCENE

Preacher Johnson withdraws from her brassiere a handful
of twenty dollar bills and flings them at him.

PREACHER JOHNSON: *Salamat*, Reverend. I've
played your mother long enough. I've been no
better than her. Nothing but a Subic Bay prostitute.

Pacquino explodes, slapping her, knocking her down.
Preacher Johnson looks up, horrified and sobbing to see
her congregation follow him out the door.

EXT. WAR MEMORIAL PLAZA - DAY

A mob of a few thousand, THE ORANGE ARRAY,
occupies the City Hall steps. Some carry flags of "Western
Maryland." Most wear orange camouflage-patterned
shirts.

Dayton and Pacquino glad-hand among them. A Mini
Cooper pulls in. Lasuli steps out, carrying a bullhorn.
Breathless.

LASULI: You've got support! Platform Member
Reid, like, so did not run off... from the chlorine?
She stayed, yeah... To demand... that the
Governor... will, I mean, respond? To the terrorists?
The terrorists. Like... closing down the Platform...
Like, state control of Baltimore!

Shouts of "Hosannah!" And "Hoo-ha!"

Lasuli drops the bullhorn, letting other cheerleaders take over. She walks over to Dayton.

>DAYTON: Aren't you the rabble rouser.

Pacquino joins them, intervening and unwelcome.

>PACQUINO: My people are ready. For action. From the heart. Not from taxpayers' pockets.

>DAYTON: No police? No firemen? No EMTs...? Oh, never mind.

>PACQUINO (rapturously insipid): The Manifest's orange sun is shining through! The golden light... of the Movement... for Repentance.

>DAYTON (distastefully): My people are different than yours.

Pacquino turns away, miffed.

INT. CHAMBER OF THE PEOPLE'S PLATFORM - SAME DAY

The chamber is full.

>THE CHAIR: The Chair recognizes the member from District Eleven.

>TURK: Threats bring people together. But they also force them into clans. Some citizens, as you all have heard, think this Platform is, itself, poison.

>SYLVIA: We are facing an insurrection that goes beyond the borders of our city. This group outside is armed and is organizing a march.

TURK: Citizens who support the democratic order, who support our Peoples Platform, are gathering at Patterson Park.

A rude clamor interrupts as a dozen orange-clad men and women stomp into the chamber. Their t-shirts carry the logo of "The Orange Array."

THE ORANGE ARRAY: Competent people of the city, throw off your chains! Obliterate the ordinary! Down with the wimps!

The Chair calls for the police who, despite the ensuing melee, arrest all of the disrupters.

EXT. WAR MEMORIAL PLAZA - NEXT DAY

Late afternoon, The Orange Array militia has defiantly parked a couple of Humvees on the grass. Pacquino, Dayton and Lasuli address the assembled media. One after the other.

DAYTON (circumspect): Randomness or merit? The populace doesn't know what it wants.

PACQUINO (hyped up): We are the spearhead! To focus! To strive! To move! To original principles. With leadership. Inspired leadership.

LASULI (crafty): My boss, Member Reid, believes in transparency. Like... Not that obfuscation stuff? An elected council would never, like... have gotten this far, this bad?

DAYTON (constrained, duplicitous): No one asked the Minute Men at Concord and Lexington. To do. What they knew. They had to do.

As afternoon light begins to fade, the militia retreats to Druid Hill Park.

EXT. DRUID HILL PARK – LATER

Encampment of The Orange Array. Pacquino, Dayton and Lasuli address the militia, unarmed except for a couple of hunting rifles.

      DAYTON (perfunctory): Disarray demands array.

      THE ORANGE ARRAY: Array! Array! Array!

      PACQUINO (rabid): The nation's salvation!

      THE ORANGE ARRAY: Salvé! Salvé! Salvé!

      LASULI (jocular): You guys are, like, getting pretty good at that.

She high-fives a couple of close-bys.

      LASULI (CONT'D): The people want class. Like, that's what we are. I mean, a class act?

The crowd murmurs uneasily. Is it humor?

      DAYTON (rote): The people want stability. Leadership.

      PACQUINO: You are learning! What Oneness is! What Unity can be!

      LASULI (aside to DAYTON): Like... what a simple-minded sheepfold can be... But aren't we showing them?

DAYTON (soberly): What will it take? Nearly three centuries since the city's founding... Still counting.

EXT. DRUID HILL PARK - NEXT DAY

The Orange Array streams out of its encampment and down Calvert Street toward City Hall. Pacquino, animated, and DAYTON, stately, up front. Jill Lasuli lags, then slinks away from the group.

EXT. PATTERSON PARK - CONTINUOUS

The Confederates' Contingent pour out of the park, parading over Baltimore Avenue toward City Hall. Many hoist placards of a green butterfly.

At the head of the march -- with purpose and determination -- Turk, Sanjit, Sylvia and Organizer stride. And Clara rolls under her own steam.

EXT. WAR MEMORIAL PLAZA - CONTINUOUS

Phalanxes of riot police ring the plaza.

The Orange Array turns into the western side of the Plaza. The Confederates' Contingent turns into the eastern side. Face off.

Mayor Dayton and Reverend Pacquino separate from the crowd, walking to the entrance of City Hall.

Accompanying them are Crisanto and Bayani, both in Orange Array uniform. They carry the aluminum box which Crisanto had prepared at Fort Detrick.

Turk and Sylvia separate from the Confederates' Contingent and move towards the City Hall entrance. Sanjit wheels Clara close behind.

The two groups of four face off at the doors of City Hall.

> PACQUINO (drooling, maniacal): By any means The Manifest deems necessary!

> DAYTON (to Pacquino, taunting): Where's the line?

> SYLVIA: Shame? Would it be shame?

> TURK: Or old-time religious flimflam?

Sylvia, Turk and the Confederates' Contingent raise their arms heavenward.

Pacquino rages in anger and disgust. He pulls a key from his pocket and inserts it into the box.

> DAYTON (smirking, to Pacquino): The line, Reverend?

> PACQUINO (utterly insane): Believers will survive! The Manifest protects the righteous!

> DAYTON (snide): That so? You, too, an aesthete of decay? And, oh, of course, transformation.

Pacquino turns the key to the box. It will not turn.

> DAYTON (CONT'D): No line. No price too great... Reverend?

Sylvia drops to her knees, hands in prayer.

> PACQUINO: *Tsch!* Apostasy! *Tsch!* Heresy! *Tsch!* Heathenism! *Tsch-tsch-tsch!*

Pacquino struggles, trying to open the locked box. Dayton pulls a key from his pocket and hands it to Pacquino.

Pacquino stares at the key, crazed.

DAYTON (taunting): Afraid, Reverend?

Pacquino tries DAYTON's key. It works. Pacquino removes the stoppered flask marked "Infectious Substance, Category A, Affecting Humans."

DAYTON (CONT'D) (openly hostile): The Manifest protects the righteous, does it?

Dayton notices himself rubbing his green emerald ring. Everything freezes for him.

EXT. PRIVATE BOY'S HIGH SCHOOL – DAY

DAYTON'S MEMORY

Still the 1920's. In the company of the white manager of the swimming pool, Dayton's grandfather is being introduced to the headmaster of an exclusive boy's high school.

BACK TO SCENE

DAYTON (pointing to the flask): No seventeen hertz here, Apocalypse. Would you really?

Pacquino's body shakes violently. With great determination he controls himself enough to smash the flask onto the ground. He collapses.

Crisanto and Bayani flee. Pandemonium seizes all of their Orange Array compatriots.

DAYTON (CONT'D) (to those fleeing): No! No! Don't...

Dayton waves, starts to run after them. But quickly gives up, hopeless to stop them. He walks slowly away, unconcerned, leaving Pacquino behind, prone and unconscious.

Sylvia, Turk, Clara and Sanjit and the Confederates' Contingent drift away, uncertain and confused.

EXT. MOUNT VERNON PLACE - DAYS LATER - DAY

Autumn colors in full glory. Turk and Sylvia relax in the shadow of Baltimore's Washington Monument.

> TURK: I thought the toughest thing would be boredom. Meetings.
>
> SYLVIA: Life on the inside. Fluorescents.
>
> TURK: Two years to go.
>
> SYLVIA: We are ready now.

INT. "RUTH'S DINER" - DAY

Sign on the door: "Closed." Television is off. Ruth and Sanjit sit in a booth over coffees.

> RUTH: So, Aggie... Game over? The Mayor turns traitor to his own cause?
>
> SANJIT: He never was an acolyte. How he managed to substitute a decoy, we may never know. I guess it was his way of being a patriot.
>
> RUTH: Breaking the rules.
>
> SANJIT: Random loves sports, isn't that the way?
>
> RUTH: So, now y'all can get to the city's business.

Sanjit nods assent.

> RUTH (CONT'D): You were talking about an investigative trip. Or was it just a vacation in some wilderness?

> SANJIT: Wilderness? Wild is any place with creatures that can kill you.

> RUTH: Oh? Then stay here in the city.

> SANJIT: With wild... comes free.

INT. OFFICE OF MAYOR DAYTON: - DAY

From behind his desk, Dayton endures Lasuli.

> LASULI: So what's next, for you, Mayor? So you saved the republic, this little city-state? You want a medal? Or maybe the starring role in a movie? Cincinnatus, like?

> DAYTON: Ah, Lasuli... It's about how you play the game. I guess I ought to walk the streets with a sign: The End Is Near. (sighs) Mine.

> LASULI: What about my cut? My choice cut.

Dayton waves dismissively. He displays his ring.

> DAYTON: Granddaddy's legacy.

He removes the ring and hands it to her.

> DAYTON (CONT'D): Corrosion's coruscations. Exquisite. Endlessly fascinating.

Lasuli beholds the gem.

DAYTON (CONT'D): Not the same kind of power, though, is it...? As power corrupts and absolute power...

LASULI: No, it ain't. Besides, minerals ain't organic? Don't corrupt. Or grow, like, and kill all friggin' life on the planet?

DAYTON: Transform, then. Decay. Corrupt. All the same.

Dayton's had enough of her. He rises, hands her a sheaf of papers.

DAYTON (CONT'D): Your documents of expungement. Consider...

She returns the ring.

LASULI: The arrest? I'm clean?

DAYTON: Clean? Have you not learned anything?

He escorts her to the door.

DAYTON (CONT'D): Excuse my humor but... For you, the prospective real estate mogul: Mold sold! Goodbye, my dear Miss Louche Lasuli.

INT. SUV TAXI - A MONTH LATER - DAY

An early winter snow flurry. Turk, Sanjit, Sylvia and Clara taxi toward City Hall.

SANJIT: Sortition. One leg of democracy. For accurate representation.

CLARA: The electoral franchise, the other.

SYLVIA: A fully representative democracy, two legs.

CLARA: As the mayor put it... Choice.

The taxi pulls up to the City Hall doors.

TURK: Speaking of which... May I choose to have a dance?

As they exit the taxi, amid the falling snow, Turk takes Cathy's hand and twirls it high. Sanjit and Clara do a wheelchair pas de deux.

CREDITS SCROLL OVER – DAYS LATER

Sanjit in a barn at Pimlico race track, practicing with the "Hands" how to twirl a lasso.

Sylvia in a greenhouse at USDA's Genetic Improvement for Fruits & Vegetables Laboratory in Beltsville, Maryland. She is examining seed trials of perennial grains.

Turk in the Enoch Pratt public library, ensconced in tomes of research about wind turbines.

Clara in a high school gym, playing in a game of wheelchair basketball.

SUPER: "MOTION TO ADJOURN"

== THE END ==

About the author

David Grant has dedicated over four decades to
political, cultural and community affairs.
Among his accomplishments, in chronological
order, are: Master of Fine Arts at the Iowa Writer's
Workshop; public television producer-director; self-
sufficient homesteading; Peace Corps agro-forester
among hunter-gatherers in the Philippines;
community organizer with Rural Southern Voice for
Peace, developing "The Listening Project"; founder
of "Peace Troupe" theater group; educator and
trainer in nonviolence for the International
Fellowship of Reconciliation; charter director of
Nonviolent Peaceforce; founder of Common Lot
Productions, exploring improved forms of
democracy.

www.commonlotproductions.net

www.ingramcontent.com/pod-product-compliance
Lightning Source LLC
Chambersburg PA
CBHW032115280326

41933CB00009B/856